Are You Saved?

Books by Thomas H. Troeger

PUBLISHED BY THE WESTMINSTER PRESS

*Are You Saved? Answers to the Awkward
Question*

Meditation: Escape to Reality

*Rage! Reflect. Rejoice! Praying with the
Psalmists*

Are You Saved?
Answers to the Awkward Question

Thomas H. Troeger

W'
The Westminster Press
Philadelphia

First edition

Published by The Westminster Press ®
Philadelphia, Pennsylvania

PRINTED IN THE UNITED STATES OF AMERICA

9 8 7 6 5 4 3 2 1

Library of Congress Cataloging in Publication Data

Troeger, Thomas H   1945–
    Are you saved?

    1. Salvation. I. Title.
BT751.2.T76   234   79-14402
ISBN 0-664-24267-7

Contents

Chapter 1

Are You Saved?

"It gives me the creeps when anyone asks, 'Are you saved?' "

The speaker was a faithful Presbyterian. His statement will strike people in different ways.

Individuals who have had an intense personal encounter with Christ may read the man's words as confirmation of what they have believed all along: the established churches do not preach the gospel. Rather, they offer an amalgamation of politics, popular culture, psychology, and personal opinion. Anyone who blushes at salvation has obviously not understood the good news of Jesus Christ.

But individuals who are reserved about expressing their faith may identify with the man's words. If they are confronted on the street or at a party by someone who wants to "save" them, they feel as though they have been handed a stick of dynamite. Their first reaction is to defuse the thing and lay it calmly down before it explodes into a testimonial. They make a polite attempt to listen for a minute but then try to steer the conversation toward a more comfortable topic.

Neither fervent proclamation nor embarrassed silence is an adequate response to the man who gets "the creeps" about salvation. Evangelizing

8 ARE YOU SAVED?

will turn him off. Saying nothing will help him to hide from a fundamental question about life.

Two Kinds of Embarrassment

"Are you saved?"

The question can be embarrassing for two reasons. First of all, despite the modern plea for openness, many individuals hold it as an article of faith that religion is a highly private matter. A stranger in their bedroom presents no greater invasion of their privacy than someone's asking, "Are you saved?" There are certain rooms in a person's psychic home that none but the most intimate acquaintances may enter. Religion is one of them.

Jesus himself favored a certain modesty in religious matters. He counseled against practicing our piety before others (Matt. 6:1ff.). The man with "the creeps" should feel no judgment because of his reserve. To interpret such modesty as the recalcitrance of sin is to reduce salvation to the psychological category of interpersonal openness. Salvation involves something much grander than the style of one's personality. Modesty in matters of belief can be an act of discipleship. It can be a way of faithfully following him who promised that our "Father who sees in secret will reward you" (Matt. 6:4).

There is, however, another possible cause for the man's embarrassment. This one takes us into the profoundest depths of the self and the farthest dimensions of salvation. It is the burglar alarm that sounds when the interior vaults of the self are broken into and entered by holy truth. The question of salvation can rob people of their complacency. It can drill through the strongbox where they keep locked up their illusions of immortality and self-perfection. It can reveal their vulnerability and show how naked they are before God.

This deeper form of embarrassment causes the heart and not just the face to blush. It is what Adam and Eve felt when they heard God walking in the garden and "hid themselves from the presence of the Lord God among the trees of the garden" (Gen. 3:8).

SALVATION AS A RELIGIOUS ANTIQUE

Unfortunately, the question "Are you saved?" awakens in many contemporary persons the first type of embarrassment without engaging the second. "Salvation" sounds like such an ancient religious word that it no longer appears to connect with the daily life of people. To use a phrase of Emily Dickinson's, the word does not penetrate to "Where the Meanings, are." It fails to hook up with the way most people organize and understand the world. Therefore, "salvation" lacks the power to disturb persons at the deepest level of their existence, to make them uneasy about themselves and their values.

"Salvation" may be an impotent term even for Christians who use it without any sense of awkwardness. When pressed to explain what it means to be saved, they frequently fall back on parallel religious phrases: "born again," "made new by the Spirit," "accept Jesus Christ as Lord and Savior." The result is that salvation sounds like the rite of some secret religious fraternity—a lovely, warm experience for those who undergo it, but essentially unrelated to the larger world.

How can people who live in the age of computers, direct distance dialing, organ transplants, and instant breakfasts hear again the question, "Are you saved?" How can they react with more than awkwardness to its antiquated sound? How can they be shaken by its contemporary significance?

The answer is to raise the issue of salvation in a form that is both comprehensible to the modern mind and faithful to its ancient meaning. By understanding salvation in the context of the human and historical situations where it appears in the Bible, we may discern how salvation continues to be an authentic concern for our age.

Salvation confronts us in a variety of ways that go unnoticed because we have such a limited understanding of the word. We need to realize that the issue of salvation is implicitly present in the texture of our common life: when we pay a premium on our life insurance policy; when we experience political upheaval; when we purchase a book on dieting or self-improvement; when we react to the welfare system; when we accept someone's apology; when we vote on an environmental bond issue; when we break the silence with a stranger at a party. Unless we can relate salvation to these concerns, it will represent nothing more than the eloquence of the preacher—appropriate in the pulpit but worthless in the everyday world. The language of salvation will continue to sound like the lyrics of a love song that once was popular but whose sentiment now appears mawkish and quaint.

If, however, we recognize salvation to be as pressing an issue as the purity of our drinking water or the human dimensions of unemployment, then we may no longer be socially embarrassed by the question "Are you saved?" We may get more than "the creeps." We may discover the bedrock assumptions of our lives crumbling like paper plates in a campfire.

Salvation Today

This book is an effort to find synonyms for salvation, to locate words, phrases, and experiences that can reach us "Where the Meanings, are."

The book is rooted in the life of a congregation I served as pastor. Many members of the church were upset because individuals were asking them at the shopping center and downtown: "Are you saved?" Some parish children were told that their baptisms were worthless.

No one knew quite how to react.

The members of the congregation sensed that salvation is central to their belief, but they were vague about what it means. The Christians who were pressuring them for a new commitment were not helpful. They relied on more abstruse religious phrases to describe what already seemed like a theological conundrum. They interpreted salvation as "accepting Jesus as one's personal Savior." This was no help at all, because the word "savior" is a cognate of salvation, and its meaning is equally opaque.

It is irresponsible discipleship to confront people with religious language that we cannot clearly interpret to them. That is laying a burden on them too hard to carry (Matt. 23:4). The letter of I Peter instructs us: "Be ready at all times to answer anyone who asks you to explain the hope you have in you" (3:15, Today's English Version). It is no explanation to talk in circles: "To be saved is to accept Jesus as Savior, which means he is the one who saves us."

Calling Jesus "Savior" is like the final chord in a classical symphony. We need to have heard the

earlier themes and variations in order to appreci-
ate the composer's resolution. The chord without
the symphony is reduced to a meaningless, solitary
sound. The symphony without the chord is trun-
cated; it leaves the music unresolved and the lis-
tener dissatisfied.

When we call Jesus "Savior," the themes and
variations of the Old Testament should be ringing
inside us. We need to hear the bass figures of God's
Spirit moving through the fugues of history, the
brassy declarations of the prophets, and the melo-
dies of the psalmists.

This book attempts to make the claim that
"Jesus is Savior" sound with power in the ears of
modern listeners. It replays the original themes of
salvation as we first hear them in the Old Testament. It then traces their development, recapitula-
tion, and climax in the life, death, and resurrection
of Jesus Christ.

The evangelical Christians at the shopping center are raising the right question. If their preaching seems antiquated, at least they present a central Biblical issue. After all, the gospel *is* about
salvation, a truth that many mainline churches
have irresponsibly avoided.

Now is the time to blend the faithful concern of
the evangelicals with a more contemporary theological style and analysis. People need help in identifying the relationship of salvation to their common lives. They need to see how salvation is more
than a linguistic artifact to be displayed in faith's
museum of Biblical jargon and religious talk. It is
an urgent reality demanding people's response
today.

Chapter 2

From Bondage

"Don't use the pulpit to preach politics. Just tell us about salvation."

It is a rare pastor who has never heard these or similar words. There is a common assumption that salvation and politics occupy separate worlds. Let preachers stick to saving souls and politicians to wheeling and dealing. Salvation is a personal experience, a private encounter between an individual and God. It is too precious to be smeared with the blood and sweat of the world's power struggles.

"Thus the Lord saved Israel that day from the hand of the Egyptians; and Israel saw the Egyptians dead upon the seashore" (Ex. 14:30). These words from Scripture shatter our soothing reflections on salvation. Our purely personal definition collapses. God "saved" Israel by breaking the political and military power of Egypt. Salvation for ancient Israel meant nothing less than escape to freedom. Not a place in heaven. Not a warm feeling in the heart. Not a private religious experience. But liberation from a tyrant.

Why do Christians often avoid the political meaning of salvation?

INDIVIDUALISTIC THEOLOGY

Christians believe that "God is love" (I John 4:8). Since contemporary society thinks of love in emotive and interpersonal terms, it is assumed that God's love must be known primarily through individual experience and relationships to other people. There is some truth to this assumption. The Gospels give us clear pictures of God's love reaching to individuals.

But the Bible does not limit God's love to interpersonal relationships. Love embraces far more than feeling. Love extends through and beyond both individuals and the world. The exodus was an act of love on God's part. Moses told the Israelites: "It is because the Lord loves you, and is keeping the oath which he swore to your fathers, that the Lord has brought you out with a mighty hand, and redeemed you from the house of bondage, from the hand of Pharaoh king of Egypt" (Deut. 7:8).

The corporate and political character of God's love eludes many people because popular culture constructs its universe around the individual. The highest value is self-fulfillment, and the journey of faith has become the attempt to find oneself.

The opposite is true in the Bible.

God is the focus of the universe. The highest value is to empty ourselves in obedience to our common Lord (Phil. 2:5ff.), and the journey of faith is the life of a pilgrim moving toward God's Promised Land (Heb. 11:13ff.).

The way we construct our world view determines the size and shape of our understanding of salvation. If we center on the self, then salvation shrinks from public event to private experience, from divine revelation to human insight, from historical significance to personal meaning.

Our shriveled conception of salvation is apparent in the very way we approach the topic: "Are you saved?" The question is too subjective. It presupposes that salvation is synonymous with a conscious feeling of having been saved. This emphasis on inner awareness to the exclusion of outward event would puzzle the ancient Israelites who recorded the stories of the exodus. If we asked them, "Are you saved?" they would recount once again how the Hebrew slaves escaped from Pharaoh. And while they imagined the floating debris of the Egyptian army, they might repeat the words of Miriam's celebration: "Sing to the Lord, for he has triumphed gloriously; the horse and his rider he has thrown into the sea" (Ex. 15:21).

Miriam's song is more than the exultant cry of a victor, and the exodus is more than a political act. Both point beyond the escape from Egypt to God who loves us through the upheavals of history as well as through the rebirth of individuals.

WHAT WE SEE AND HEAR

The first step in connecting salvation to "Where the Meanings, are" is to rephrase our question. No longer do we ask, "Are you saved?" (At a later point we will return to consider when this question is appropriate.) Instead, we put the matter this way: "Do you see how God is at work liberating people in the world?" We shift from looking inward to looking outward. We seek our Lord not among our feelings but among our fellow human beings.

Jesus himself teaches that our reaction to external demands is a truer measurement of salvation

than religious feeling. In his parable of the sheep
and the goats (Matt. 25:31ff.), the standard of judgment has absolutely nothing to do with inner
awareness. God welcomes to the Kingdom those
who, without giving a thought to what it would
earn them in heaven, have been feeding, clothing,
and visiting the wretched of the earth. But God
rejects those who were presumptuous enough to
think they had it made: "Lord, when did we see
thee hungry or thirsty or a stranger or naked or sick
or in prison, and did not minister to thee?" (Matt.
25:44).

The parable is more than a powerful call to compassion. It is a severe warning to any Christian who
says to another person, "Are you saved?" We may
be sinfully cocky in asking the question, and the
person we address may be faithfully humble in not
being able to respond. The parable reminds us that
God is the judge. Certainty of our own goodness is
a hot tip that we are among the damned! The mark
of the saved is that they leave judgment in God's
hands while they serve the world with their own.

We still witness to how God saves people. But the
basis of our testimony is no longer primarily ourselves or others' awareness. We focus on the world
of human events and on God who is at work there.

Even in evaluating his own ministry, Jesus ap-
pealed to external events. When John the Baptist
sent his disciples to ask Jesus, "Are you he who is
to come, or shall we look for another?" (Matt. 11:3),
Jesus did not respond by discussing his inner state.
He did not probe his consciousness. He did not describe feelings of intense closeness to God or give
accounts of spiritual ecstasies that had swept his
soul. Rather, Jesus pointed to the way the world is
being healed: "Go and tell John what you hear and
see: the blind receive their sight and the lame walk,

lepers are cleansed and the deaf hear, and the dead are raised up, and the poor have good news preached to them. And blessed is he who takes no offense at me" (Matt. 11:4-6). Notice how Jesus, instead of saying, "I give the blind their sight," says, "The blind receive their sight." This puts the emphasis on God's healing power. If Jesus is this self-effacing in his testimony, then disciples must make sure that their witness to salvation puts the lightest touch on themselves and the greatest accent on God.

We find the substance of salvation in what we hear and see. Since television news is the most popular medium for hearing and seeing the world, we must consider it one of the prime locations for making connections between salvation and contemporary life.

"The news is the atmosphere of what we see and hear and almost breathe, and it is often excessively polluted and depressing, but it is still an important part of the truth." (James Reston, *The New York Times,* Sept. 5, 1975.)

Salvation as liberation encourages us to peer through the polluted atmosphere of the news. When Walter Cronkite concludes with the words "That's the way it is," we know that's not the way it is *completely.* We do not dispute that the events we see are true: the car overturned in the street and set on fire, the distended stomach, the unemployment line, the politician's unctuous grin. We view them all, and we are convinced "That's the way it is."

But we are also convinced of something else. We believe that the sum total of the news of history shall reveal that in the fiercest human events a power is present who seeks to free all people. As "the Lord saved Israel that day from the hand of the Egyptians," so the Lord continues to rescue people from bondage.

"That's the way it is."

Yes, dark and bitter and red with blood, just as our solid-state, extra-fine color-tuned televisions show us. But the world is also buoyant with God's power for salvation.

SALVATION AS NEWS COMMENTARY

Salvation is the ultimate news commentary. It traces the underlying cause of human events to God who is working in, through, and beneath the struggle of people to claim their freedom. Salvation puts the news in perspective. We no longer react simply on the basis of fear or self-interest. Our knee-jerk behavior, as either conservative or middle of the road or liberal or radical, ceases. The assurance of God's presence in world events calms our panic.

A theological slant on the news stirs the desire for a politically informed faith. Private belief is an inadequate response to God when we understand that God is working in the larger world of politics and conflict. Loyalty to God demands participation with God in the struggles of the world.

DISTORTIONS OF SALVATION

There is danger in a political understanding of salvation. It is easily distorted by our assuming that God is on our side. Our cause becomes holy, and we disguise our shortcomings and compromises in the armor of the crusader. The politician plays priest, and ideology masquerades as divine truth. Instead of liberation we end up with the worst kind of enslavement: political expediency that claims to be ordained and blessed by God.

The authors of this parody of salvation come from every point on the political spectrum. There are conservatives who present the free market as an essential structure of the universe. There are liberals who usher in new programs as though they are the Kingdom of God. There are revolutionaries who hold to a naive utopianism.

The flaw in all parodies of salvation as liberation is their messianism. They point to themselves rather than to God. They assert that their ideas, their programs, their leaders are the ultimate answer to the riddles of society. The Christian faith punctures these pretensions with its belief that the Messiah has already come.

JESUS CHRIST LIBERATES US

When we say, "Jesus Christ is our Savior," we are acknowledging that he is our liberator. But how does Jesus free us? Is it being honest to the Gospel portraits of Jesus to see him as a political liberator? Christians crash head on with one another in answering these questions.

Some faithful believers, most notably the liberation theologians, choose Luke 4:16ff. to assert that Jesus defined his ministry in terms of freeing those in bondage. By reading from Isaiah's call "to proclaim release to the captives" and "to set at liberty those who are oppressed," Jesus was announcing the revolutionary character of his own mission. Luke 4:16ff. becomes a proof text for the contention that the gospel is primarily about political liberation.

What then about Jesus' healing the Roman centurion's slave (Matt. 8:5-13; Luke 7:1-10)? The
Roman centurion was the oppressor. If Jesus were
a political liberator, why did he not deliver to the
soldier a revolutionary manifesto? Why instead did
Jesus praise the man as he did few other people in
the Gospel?

I am deliberately setting text against text to dem-
onstrate the futility of trying to prove one image of
Jesus over the other. Yes, there are passages where
Jesus stands straight in line with the Old Testament prophets and their demands for social justice. Yes, there are also passages where he deals in
a personal way with people that transcends every
human distinction, even that between oppressor
and oppressed. Yet greater than these individual
snapshots of the prophet and the pastor, greater
than his specific examples and teaching is Jesus
himself. To understand how Jesus frees us requires
more than finding Biblical stories that describe his
liberating activity. It demands knowing who Jesus
Christ is.

There are a number of New Testament texts that
proclaim Christ's universal significance. Although
no statement captures the totality of who he is,
there is a passage that particularly illuminates our
understanding of Christ as liberator: "Think not
that I have come to abolish the law and the prophets; I have come not to abolish them but to fulfil
them" (Matt. 5:17). Whether these are the words of
Jesus or the church's attempt to interpret Jesus'
purpose, they show that Christ does not abnegate
the political salvation which we find in the Old
Testament. He represents the completion of that
liberating activity.

The modern propensity to debate whether Jesus'
salvation is personal or societal imposes a dichot-

omy that is native to our way of thinking but alien to the New Testament. In the verses that follow Jesus' claim to fulfill the law and the prophets (Matt. 5:18-48), Jesus gives examples of personal righteousness. They deal with the treatment of brothers, wives, neighbors, and enemies. However, a personalistic reading of these passages ignores the context of Jesus' teaching. Jesus keeps referring to the general understanding of the society in which he speaks, to the regulations of Jewish tradition. Hence, the repeated formula: "You have heard that it was said." Jesus directs his teaching toward the transformation of a corporate rather than a private perception of what God requires. Although what he says has ramifications for individuals, he aims beyond private actions to the greater purpose which God has revealed in "the law and the prophets." The most important event in that revelation is the exodus. Jesus interprets his teaching as the dynamic completion of God's saving people through political liberation. For Jesus there is no tension between political and personal salvation. Each is related to the other. Both are evidence of God's power to free us.

To present Jesus' instruction without the political thrust of the Old Testament is like giving someone a tree to plant without its roots. Private religion withers and dies when there is not a mutually nourishing relationship with the political aspects of God's activity.

Our Savior does not work in a laboratory for spiritual research where everyone is dressed in white robes of piety and is registering the results of the latest religious experience or measuring the intensity of prayer. Scripture does not say, "God so loved the sanctuary," but "God so loved the world." Our Savior lives amid the Molotov cocktail, the smoke-filled room, the tenement with the leaking toilet, the child bitten by the rat, the political prisoner shocked with an electric cattle prod. If we abandon the world, then we are deserting Jesus just as the disciples did in the Garden. They shared the meal, but they did not share the cross.

To accept Jesus as our Savior is to receive the strength to face the world. Christ's presence empowers us to participate in the political liberation that God is bringing about. Our social activism is more than a penchant for identifying with every cause and movement. It is the commitment of disciples who embrace their Lord by reaching out to the world.

Christ is no longer simply *"my* Savior." Such a claim treats Christ as though he were a private possession, a figure of porcelain piety stored in devotion's cupboard where there is no threat of shattering him against the concrete terrors of history.

An individual's decision to accept Christ means to recognize Christ as the *world's* Savior. The acknowledgment of Christ's Lordship is a personal act. But the truth that the individual affirms is transpersonal, extending far beyond the boundary of the self. The disciple senses Christ's liberating presence in the outrage of conscience, in the demand for equality, in the resolve never to bend the soul to the state, in the revolt of the exploited and the oppressed, in the refusal to swallow a party line, in the remembrance of what we owe God as well as what we owe Caesar (Matt. 22:21). These rebellions against the illegitimate claims of human authority are evidences of Christ's continual liberating activity.

Even when he is not mentioned by name, Christ is secretly present. Beneath the human demand for freedom lies the divine drive for liberation.

Our confidence in Christ's presence transforms our response to a world in upheaval: no longer panic but courage, no longer retreat but involvement, no longer overconsumption but sharing. We have not received "the spirit of slavery to fall back into fear, but [we] have received the spirit of sonship" (Rom. 8:15). The pharaohs of earth have been replaced by "Our Father, who art in heaven." We are not the slaves of a tyrant but the children of a loving parent.

Our lives explain to the world what it means to believe that "Jesus Christ is our Savior." It is no longer an awkward, antiquated confession. It is the central principle of existence, which steadies us in the face of violence, which sustains us in the struggle for justice, and which judges and renews our politics. Together with Christ as our Savior we confront the forces that enslave people. We know that someday even "the creation itself will be set free from its bondage to decay and obtain the glorious liberty of the children of God" (Rom. 8:21).

Chapter 3

From Insecurity

The thunder of iron chariots and the war whoop of attacking tribes had replaced the snap of the whip. The Hebrews were settling into Canaan. They were no longer slaves. The exodus and the wilderness wandering were behind them. Now their most urgent concern was protection from hostile neighbors.

"Then the Lord raised up judges, who saved them out of the power of those who plundered them. . . . Whenever the Lord raised up judges for them, the Lord was with the judge, and he saved them from the hand of their enemies all the days of the judge" (Judg. 2:16,18).

The same God who had liberated the Hebrews from Egypt made them secure in Canaan. Just as the anguish of their slavery had moved God to free them (Ex. 3:7-8), so God responded out of compassion to their new plight: "The Lord was moved to pity by their groaning because of those who afflicted and oppressed them" (Judg. 2:18). God had not broken Pharaoh's shackles in order to enslave the people to constant terror. Liberation that leads to anarchy is not salvation. To be saved means to be made secure as well as free.

FAITH IN TEDDY BEARS

"But whenever the judge died, they turned back
and behaved worse than their fathers, going after
other gods, serving them and bowing down to
them; they did not drop any of their practices or
their stubborn ways" (Judg. 2:19). In the absence of
a leader clearly chosen by God, the Israelites
turned to the symbols of power offered by the surrounding culture. They "went after other gods,
from among the gods of the peoples who were
round about them, and bowed down to them"
(Judg. 2:12).

Faith in bogus securities. That was the pattern
in ancient Palestine, and that is the pattern of people's lives whenever they do not see a sure sign of
God's presence. Like small children in a bedroom
who cling to stuffed animals when their parents
leave, the peoples of the world grab on to leaders,
causes, prejudices, ideologies, values, possessions,
and weapons to fill the vacuum of God's absence.
Anything not to be alone. False gods are better than
no god. Eventually people come to believe that
their god is the one true God. Again like children in
the bedroom, they find that they can go to sleep.
They feel secure, but they are not saved.

Jesus knew how people curl up beside the
teddy bears of wealth and position while they
forget the parent who bore them, raised them,
and watched over them. In his parable about the
rich farmer Jesus tries to rouse us from our somnolent security: " 'Fool! This night your soul is
required of you; and the things you have prepared, whose will they be?' So is he who lays up
treasure for himself, and is not rich toward God"

(Luke 12:20-21). The parable affirms the joy of being extravagant toward God. The farmer's problem is that he hoarded his goods to guarantee his security. His wizened little world rather than his wealth is what Jesus ridicules.

Christ's own life is a reversed image parable of his story about the fat cat farmer: "For you know the grace of our Lord Jesus Christ, that though he was rich, yet for your sake he became poor, so that by his poverty you might become rich" (II Cor. 8:9). The pattern of our lives is not to be inward, anxious, and miserly, but outward, confident, and generous.

We are like the bottom bulb of an hourglass. All our lives people have been funneling care and strength into us. From our mothers' milk to the books in the public library we have depended on someone else's presence and knowledge. It is for ourselves as well as for the Lord that a way has been prepared in the wilderness (Isa. 40:3). Before we were born battles were fought, experiments were performed, music was composed, wisdom was gained, and the spare room was cleaned and stocked with diapers and a bassinet. We have received and received and received.

The greatest threat in the world is to turn the hourglass upside down, to reverse the flow, to pour ourselves out. It requires altering our security reflexes. Try to punch a man. His hands and arms will guard his body in an instant. In a similar fashion we clutch inside when we are told as children to share our candy with our friend or as adults to redistribute our wealth among the dispossessed of the earth.

How can we invert the mold of our existence and find security in giving as well as receiving?

JESUS CHRIST MAKES US SECURE

Salvation means to be turned upside down so that all the love and nurture that God has poured into us now pours out of us into the world. Jesus Christ inverts us through his teaching, through his relationship to us, and through the way he reconstructs reality.

Teaching alone will never change our essential nature. Relationship and experience transform our character more forcefully than instruction. Nevertheless, Christ's teaching is often the first beachhead he uses to invade our false sense of security. Even the prettiest verses have a way of starting an earthquake within us by breaking through our assumptions.

"Consider the lilies of the field, how they grow; they neither toil nor spin; yet I tell you, even Solomon in all his glory was not arrayed like one of these" (Matt. 6:28-29). What lovely poetry this is until we discover that Jesus is not talking about the flowers that bloom in the spring. He is examining the kind of anxiety that strikes us when we lose our credit rating. "If God so clothes the grass of the field, which today is alive and tomorrow is thrown into the oven, will he not much more clothe you, O men of little faith?" (Matt. 6:30). Tell that to the bank. Take your lilies and try to pay the car loan and the grocer with them. Better to read Sylvia Porter than the Sermon on the Mount if you want to straighten out your finances.

For Jesus, the lily is a proclamation to the world that things are not as they appear. We think that wealth and power would guarantee our security. How splendid to be a king like Solomon, with stables of horses, a reputation for wisdom, an opulent palace, and visits from exotic and beautiful women! But this lily standing in the same field with the manure and the puddles from last night's rain is dressed more elegantly than Solomon in his coronation gown.

To see a flower and know that the same hand which painted its petals is knitting together molecules to form the cells of our body is shattering. Shattering because it calls into question all of our striving for security: the long commute to live in the right neighborhood, the late office hours to get ahead of our associate, the vote for the candidate who promises that our country will always be number one. Jesus calls all of these into question with a lily. He turns a flower into a Declaration of Independence, announcing that we no longer need to stake our security on the values and status symbols of the world. God and God alone is the guarantor of existence.

It is not enough to contemplate the victory of the flower. Jesus is not putting the image before us to occupy our religious reflections. His teaching demands a response: "Every one then who hears these words of mine and *does* them will be like a wise man who built his house upon the rock; and the rain fell, and the floods came, and the winds blew and beat upon that house, but it did not fall, because it had been founded on the rock" (Matt. 7:24-25, emphasis added). Here is the very picture of security. We are to build a sound home for ourselves by doing Jesus' words.

A strange expression this: doing words. It sounds wrong in English. We speak words. We write words. We read words. But we don't do words. How would we do the words about the lily?

I recall a man who once did them. We were playing a simulation game about the world's resources. Participants received different amounts of money. Then the world's resources were auctioned off. Players could buy weapons, oil, food, medicine, water, and dozens of other basic supplies as well as flowers. This one man had received the smallest sum of money, so nobody else wanted to form an alliance with him. The other participants were scrambling to buy up weapons and food in order to control the world. When the flowers of the world—represented by a single daffodil—were offered for sale, no one spoke except the man. He gave his one penny for the bloom and sat enjoying it while the game became louder and more violent.

After the game the man with the flower turned out to have the most perceptive understanding of everything that had happened. He was able to analyze who had been authoritarian, who had cheated, and how participants might have worked out a realistic peace instead of blowing up the world (as they had done!).

The man did the words of Jesus about the lily. He was not sucked into the security traps of the other participants, but achieved a discernment only possible to one who realized that "Solomon in all his glory was not arrayed like one of these."

Of course, it was only a game. It is easy to buy a daffodil and not fight for food when you are going home to lasagna after the game is finished. But try to do Christ's words in the world where petroleum, wheat, and weapons are the currency of coercion. You won't be secure then. You will be destroyed.

How can we ever find security by doing Christ's words in the real world?

THE DIVINE ACCOMPANIST

The gospel does not leave us like students in a classroom who are to complete the assignment while the teacher steps out for a break. Christ is not an idealist who spelled out high principles that subsequent generations are left to put into practice. He is the power who enables us to actualize his teaching.

Christ is like a music teacher who is master of the instrument we are struggling to play. We know that we shall never sound that good. Then our teacher shows us when to breathe, how to reshape our lips, how to move our fingers more smoothly, which notes to accent and which notes to slur. At first it is all very mechanical, and there are a lot of wrong notes and miscounted measures. We feel that we may as well give up. But our instructor asks us to play in unison. Amazing things happen! We still play wrong notes and break the phrases with faulty breathing, but the beauty of our teacher's playing carries us along. Even though we are flat on the high notes and miss the low ones, even though we cut the whole notes short, they all sound with power because our teacher is playing along with us. Our own performance takes on strength it would never possess by itself. We become more confident about our own musicianship because of the security of our teacher.

When we try to carry out Christ's teaching we do not have to worry about the inadequacy of our performance. Christ has promised that he will be acting in unison with us: "Go therefore and make disciples of all nations, baptizing them in the name of the Father and of the Son and of the Holy Spirit, teaching them to observe all that I have commanded you; and lo, I am with you always, to the close of the age" (Matt. 28:19-20). Where our words wobble and fall flat, his will sound with power. Where our love is limp, he will project his with soaring, songful beauty. Where our courage must pause to breathe, his will be sustained in long, arching phrases. To know that Christ is keeping time with us, that Christ is breathing with us, that Christ fills in the gaps of our own life is to be more secure than the concert artist who walks on stage to play the fiftieth performance of a favorite concerto. We may bungle the piece, but the concert is a guaranteed success. To know this is to be saved.

Most of our attempts to attain security are solo performances even when their aim is to provide confidence in relating to others. The how-to books, the cosmetics and deodorants, the meditation movements all aim at the solitary self. Have the right attitude. Wear the right complexion. Find inner peace. Then you will feel secure. A pimple, a change in mood, an interrupted mantra, and these routes to private salvation crumble.

Salvation in the Bible depends on nothing so flimsy as our feelings or our appearance or our acceptance by others. The Scriptures portray the Savior neither as handsome, "He had ... no beauty that we should desire him" (Isa. 53:2). Nor as happy, "My soul is very sorrowful, even to death" (Matt. 26:38). Nor as popular, "He was despised and rejected by men" (Isa. 53:3). The One who makes us secure has none of those outward marks of security which we covet. Christ saves through the strength of his presence in even the ugliest human scenes.

I remember as a seminary student making my first pastoral call on a man who had been in an automobile accident. He was in the intensive care unit. Tubes and gurgling sounds drained away the juices of my own strength. I cannot recall my words with the patient. I only know that they were brief.

As I returned over the weeks, Christ restored two patients. He healed the accident victim through the skill of the nurses and doctors. He also healed me. I was the other patient, and Christ was making me whole just as he was repairing the man's scars and broken bones. Christ was making me secure enough to relate more to the man's needs and less to my own anxiety. He subdued the fear of my own vulnerability through the struggle and victory of the person I came to visit.

Christ was the Word that sounded in those terrible silent moments when the man and I had no more human words to speak. To hear that Word when we step into a hospital room is to be saved.

And not just in a hospital room, but "wherever two or three are gathered together in [Christ's] name, [he] will be there also" (Matt. 18:20). Wherever! In the kitchen, in the asylum, in the bowling alley, in the prison, in the woods, in the slum, in the suburbs, in the hold of a ship, in the capsule of a rocket, in the sanctuary, in the locker room. Wherever people come together in Christ's name, spoken or unspoken yet present through the power of compassion and concern, wherever that takes place Christ is with us. Christ attends every get-together of the human family. To sense this in the presence of one other person or one hundred other persons is to be saved.

THE HOUSEHOLD OF GOD

Note this: Christ did not say, "Wherever a single individual is in my name, there will I be also." A minimum of two is required. This does not mean that Christ will desert us when we are alone. Rather, it indicates that Christ is known through a sharing relationship with other people.

So much of our insecurity stems from our fear of other people. We have organized the world according to our experience, our upbringing, our inherited strengths and weaknesses. We assume that our perspective on reality is reality. People who are different from us in thought and life-style threaten us because their peculiar understanding calls into question our own. To be saved is to overcome this fear. It is to realize that Christ stands among people ready to interpret their unique experiences and ways of expression.

Christ is like Georgiana, a character in the television series *Upstairs, Downstairs.* She returns to her upper-class British home during World War I to discover that a small war is taking place in the household. The Bellamys, relatives with whom she lives, have taken in a refugee family of Belgian peasants. The Bellamys hate their guests because they have rejected every act of hospitality. The refugees have spit out tea in the drawing room, have refused to take hot baths drawn for them, and have shown delight when one of their children broke a crock of jam and laughed about it. Throughout all of this no one offers a word of explanation, because the Bellamys speak only English and the refugees speak only French.

Georgiana, however, speaks both languages. She stands between the two families and interprets to the Bellamys the refugees' behavior. They spit out the tea because they thought it was an attempt to poison them. They refused to take a bath because they interpreted the Bellamys' gestures to mean that they must undress in front of everyone else.

They were glad when the child broke the jam crock because it was the first time he had laughed since the Germans killed his father.

Through Georgiana's translation "the walls come a tumblin' down." The refugees no longer view the Bellamys as dangerous captors. The Bellamys no longer see the refugees as hostile ingrates. The two families embrace. Reconciliation is possible because each has ceased to be a threat to the other. They are now secure enough to share their common humanity.

Christ is a translator. He speaks fluently the experience and feelings of all people. He reduces our insecurity by making the world of strangers intelligible to us. We experience his interpretive power whenever we sense a willingness to listen and to understand between ourselves and others. This willingness stems from more than psychological openness. It is rooted in the fact that Christ has restructured reality.

"For he is our peace, who has made us both one, and has broken down the dividing wall of hostility. ... And he came and preached peace to you who were far off and peace to those who were near; for through him we both have access in one Spirit to the Father" (Eph. 2:14, 17-18).

The "dividing wall of hostility" refers to the distinction between the Jews and the Gentiles. Although this historic division is no longer as pressing an issue as in the first-century church, the contrast between those who are "far off" and those who are "near" is with us in every age and in every place. There are always people who consider themselves "near"—near the mark, near authority, near the truth, near to God. They are the "ins." And there are always people who consider themselves

and are considered by others as "far off"—far off
the mark, far off from authority, far off from the
truth, far off from God. They are the "outs." Each
is estranged from the other. Each is a threat to the
other's security.

Ephesians tells us that Christ has built a structure that eliminates the "dividing wall of hostility"
between the "ins" and the "outs." "So then you are
no longer strangers and sojourners, but you are fellow citizens with the saints and members of the
household of God, built upon the foundation of the
apostles and prophets, Christ Jesus himself being
the cornerstone, in whom the whole structure is
joined together and grows into a holy temple in the
Lord; in whom you also are built into it for a dwell-
ing place of God in the Spirit" (Eph. 2:19-22).

As Georgiana's translation turns the Bellamys
and the Belgian refugees into one household, so
Christ makes the "ins" and the "outs" into fellow
citizens in the household of God. This household is
the church, not just the visible church with all its
worldly divisions but the invisible church. It is that
unseen yet indestructible connectedness which
Christians have with their Lord and with each
other even when they diverge in the details of their
religious life. The hidden church is a structural
reality in which the bricks of existence are so ar-
ranged that there are no inner walls and all are
equally supported by the chief cornerstone of Jesus
Christ.

The church is under construction. It is like an
unfinished building whose framing gives a clear
idea of its final form but whose walls are still being
built. To become a part of that building—to feel the
solidarity of its foundation and yet to wait for its
completion—is to be saved.

COFFEE HOUR COMPATIBILITY AND CHRIST'S
SECURITY

"Would you like to join our organization?"
"We are taking a bus to the state legislature to
make our feelings known on the issue. Will you
come along?"
"A contribution of five dollars makes you a mem-
ber and gives you our newsletter for a year."

Because there are so many causes and groups
that invite our participation, it is easy to think that
joining the church is simply one among many of
our social involvements. At a purely human level
there is a lot of evidence for accepting this conclusion. The church often shares with secular organi-
zations the same social distinctions of class,
wealth, race, neighborhood, and political interest.
Joining the church makes people feel secure for
the same reasons that joining any other group does:
they find there people who in values and life-style
are like themselves.

Yet the church never finds its ultimate security
in its sociological characteristics. The church is
like an old house in a suburban neighborhood
where I once lived. It had been built when the area
was first settled in the early 1800's. All the other
homes were standard ranch and split-level types.
Picture windows and aluminum siding had been
added to the old house, so that it more nearly
matched the surrounding buildings. But it did not
look right. Its outward appearance was clinging
with obvious discomfort to a frame that had much
more grace. When a couple started to restore the
house, they tore off the modern siding and discovered that the wood underneath was as solid as ever.

In all their reconstruction they tried to bring out the strength and style that lay beneath the house's exterior appearance.

Jesus Christ is the hidden frame of the visible church. His disciples may try to make the place weathertight with the wallboards of society's prejudice, but sooner or later some faithful people will tear them off and insist that the church's appearance reflects the Lord "in whom the whole structure is joined together." The church, to use the classic theological phrase, is "always reforming." It is always being rebuilt so that its human form is truer to its divine frame and foundation.

To be saved, to be made secure, through the church does not mean that we can always find someone at the coffee hour after worship who will discuss our tennis game or last night's party or Tuesday's meeting. The church is not a religious club whose charter and membership reflect the surrounding culture. To be saved is to be part of the church that is "always reforming," always attempting to be more faithful to Jesus Christ who first founded it and who continues to hold it together.

Because Christ calls into question the world's standards, the security which we find in his church is upsetting as well as calming—upsetting because it rattles our confidence in society's success symbols, calming because our lives are based on a foundation that shall never be destroyed.

CHARIOTS TO MISSILES

Neither iron chariots thundering across the plain nor intercontinental ballistic missiles aimed across the oceans have destroyed the security of

God's people. Like all human beings they tremble
at the terror that nation inflicts upon nation, and
they worry for their own earthly protection. But
beneath their fear for the world's survival is a holy
confidence that as God secured the Hebrews in Canaan, so even now God makes us secure through
Christ. To have this belief tucked into our hearts
along with our anxiety is to be saved from despair.
We work for world peace and international security because we know that even when our human
efforts falter, God's shall not. God has made us part
of his own household and is constructing our lives
and our hopes on the indestructible foundation of
Jesus Christ.

Chapter 4

From False Faith

Shouts of "Praise the Lord" and incense filled the Temple in Jerusalem. Attendance at worship was strong. Old-time religion was flourishing. The rediscovery of lost tradition and King Josiah's subsequent reforms had touched off a revival at the end of the seventh century B.C. (II Kings, chs. 22 and 23).

Yet something was rotten in Judah.

The Israelites were enslaved again. Although there was no pharaoh to hold them in his power, the new slavery was more insidious than what the Hebrews had suffered in Egypt. Its shackles and burdens were not apparent to most of the people. Only a misfit like the prophet Jeremiah perceived the nation's bondage. He realized how the revival had misfired. Israel had become captive to the forms of faith. The people worshiped in the Temple. They offered their prayers. They made their sacrifices. But theirs was a slavish observance that chained the heart to ritual rather than to compassion and subjugated the soul to habit rather than to the living God. It was a thoughtless religiosity that mixed together the worship of pagan deities with faith in the Lord.

The Israelites needed to be liberated and protected from themselves! From their arrogance, from their idolatry, from their injustice, from their unholy belief in the power of the Temple, from their thinking that they had a claim on God instead of God's having a claim on them. God had to make them into new people. Salvation required an act of creation.

THE FIRST STEP

Babylon overran Jerusalem in 587 B.C. It was an incomprehensible tragedy to most of the Israelites. The Temple had been their security blanket. So long as they could cling to it they were convinced that God was protecting them.

The Temple's destruction cracked their belief in the saving power of God. In the past, salvation had meant liberation and security. How could the conquest of the Holy Land ever be construed as an act of salvation?

The Israelites' existence as a people, which had once seemed so full of promise and purpose, had turned out to be absurd. All that talk about God's freeing them and protecting them had been nothing more than platitude. Salvation was a hoax, a nice bit of theological cotton candy to feed the priests and to make people feel good when they worshiped in the Temple. But where was God when Israel's enemies swept down on the Holy City and led the citizenry into exile? What kind of salvation were they to see amid the smoke, the charred ruins, the stabbed bodies, the plundered Temple? Let everyone who has given a testimonial to the joy of being saved keep silence before this scene. Salvation is not happy-time religion.

 Salvation is devastating. It wipes out all the false securities that we depend on for comfort and

meaning. We are not aware of how much we organize our lives around objects and symbols until they are removed from us. We assume their presence and take for granted the reassurance that they provide.

We are like an elderly couple who enjoyed fine health. It looked as though they would be able to live in their own house until they died. Since the husband was born and raised in the place, it was filled with memories. Whenever I visited them, the couple would tell me the story behind a painting, a desk, a buffet, a fireplace, a bookshelf. Then both became ill. Unable to care for themselves, they were moved to a nursing home, where they died soon after. The loss of their house with its universe of meaning killed them as much as did their ailments.

We all occupy a house filled with treasured objects: beliefs, theories, values, biases. It is our psychic home, custom decorated out of our peculiar experience and the culture in which we live. We never intend to leave. Then life changes. And just as the Israelites had to move from the Promised Land and the couple from their house, so too we must move out of the private world we cherish.

We can turn bitter.

Or we can react like Jeremiah.

While the Babylonians were building siege works up the walls of Jerusalem, Jeremiah was purchasing a piece of property from his cousin Hanamel (Jer., ch. 32). Before we buy a place, we want to know about the schools, the neighborhood, the resale value, the taxes. But here Jeremiah was taking ownership of land he would never enjoy. The purchase was a sign of God's undefeatable power. Jeremiah would never make a killing in real estate or even get to weed his field or breathe the smell of

its soil after a good rain. He knew these things. Yet
Jeremiah laid down the seventeen shekels of silver
and signed the deed. It may have been a poor business deal, but Jeremiah knew that faith is a long-
term investment. He was confident that someday
God would bring the Israelites back to the land and
"make them dwell in safety" (Jer. 32:37).

To be saved is to live knowing that there will be
a better future even when the foreseeable future is
filled with darkness. If the enemy is at the walls, if
the doctor has tried every treatment, if the peace
conference dissolves in anger, if the verdict is
"guilty," if the words are "ashes to ashes, dust to
dust," still we are not done in. God is plucking up
and breaking down in order to plant and to build up
a new reality (Jer. 31:28). What appears to be nothing but destruction is part of a process through
which God is transforming us.

REBUILDING THE DOME OF MEANING

"Thus says Cyrus king of Persia: The Lord, the
God of heaven, has given me all the kingdoms of
the earth, and he has charged me to build him a
house at Jerusalem, which is in Judah. Whoever is
among you of all his people, may his God be with
him, and let him go up to Jerusalem, which is in
Judah, and rebuild the house of the Lord, the God
of Israel" (Ezra 1:2-3).

Jeremiah turned out to be right. God had not
abandoned Israel. Babylon itself fell to the Persian
Empire, and in 538 B.C., Cyrus the Great decreed
that the captives could return and restore the Temple.

To some exiles it seemed that God was rebuilding the universe: "For behold, I create new heavens

and a new earth; and the former things shall not be remembered or come into mind. But be glad and rejoice for ever in that which I create; for behold, I create Jerusalem a rejoicing, and her people a joy" (Isa. 65:17-18). "New heavens and a new earth" may sound exaggerated when we picture what a burned-out slum Jerusalem was (Neh. 1:3). Yet such unrestrained language describes what happens whenever God rebuilds our lives.

Heaven in the Old Testament is conceived as a solid dome that arches over the earth (Gen. 1:7). The physical firmness reflects the confidence of faith: the Israelites lived under the rocklike meaning that God had built into the universe. But when the Babylonians conquered them, the sky caved in. They no longer seemed to be under God's care.

The proclamation of Cyrus the Great restored Israel's faith. It reaffirmed that God still watched over the nation. To the exiles God was rebuilding the dome of meaning: "Behold, I create new heavens and a new earth."

Although we no longer believe that the sky is a hard vault, we still want an overarching purpose to life that is as solid as heaven was to the Hebrews. We often project such significance upon an individual or upon our nation. And like the Israelites, we are terrified when the purpose that has spanned our existence crumbles. When the aunt who raised us dies, when the politician whose bumper sticker we placed on our car is convicted of grand larceny, when our nation celebrates the inalienable rights of life and liberty while exploding a neutron bomb, when God fails to act as we think God ought, then heaven's vault collapses. Life loses meaning. We become exiles in a strange land where the values we thought sacred are worthless and where the truth we held eternal is dead. Like those ancient

captives in Babylon we feel abandoned. We want
God to save us by rebuilding heaven, by restoring
the dome of meaning, by putting purpose back in
our lives.

LIFE IN CHRIST IS LIFE UNDER CHRIST

"And for anyone who is in Christ, there is a new
creation; the old creation has gone, and now the
new one is here" (II Cor. 5:17, Jerusalem Bible).
This verse is for Christians what the decree of
Cyrus the Great was for the exiles. It is a proclamation that we can return to our homeland: to God, to
love, to grace.

We have been exiles in a world where people are
estranged from one another, where the custom is to
hold every grudge, and where the only ruling
power is sheer force. Now this scary world is replaced. Or as Paul says, "the old creation has gone."
The dome of meaning that now stretches over our
lives is God's love and not humanity's hatred. This
transformation is nothing less than a "new creation." A new way of understanding life. A new way
of relating to others. A new confidence that the
meaning of existence is hopeful and not tragic. We
can speak calmly again to our neighbor whose dog
barked until 3:27 A.M. last Thursday. We can return
from our friend's funeral and weed the garden, de-
lighted at how well our lettuce and radishes are
coming. We can continue to participate in an open-
housing campaign despite the viciousness of the
opposition. All of this is possible because there is a
new creation.

"In Christ God was reconciling the world to himself" (II Cor. 5:19). God has done something to the
world and not just to individual believers. God has

transformed the nature of reality. God has changed the character of existence so that the most powerful dynamic in the universe is drawing us together rather than driving us apart.

The force of reconciliation is not apparent to everyone. It takes a deliberate act of perception to feel this force tugging on ourselves. It is something like observing the constellations that illumine the midnight sky. They go unnoticed until we turn off the late show and the porch light and gaze up from our backyard. A moment ago we were looking inside someone's sinuses and hearing a jingle for "congestion relief"; now we are looking at the Big Dipper and at interstellar spaces that exceed our comprehension. "There is a new creation." It was there before we looked, but we did not see it.

Salvation requires turning off the banality of our lives so that we can see the new creation that Christ has made. There is a heavenly glory that goes unnoticed until we put out the artificial light of our own wisdom and see the constellations of meaning that God has hung in the dark sky of existence. At first we are afraid to do this. We have lived so long with the bright lie of our own self-sufficiency that we fear that if we put it out, we will be lost in the night. It takes nothing less than a "leap of faith" to trust that when our own light is extinguished, God's "light shines in the darkness, and the darkness has not overcome it" (John 1:5).

If we make that leap of faith, then we shall discover the galaxies of God's love and hope. I have seen people do this. I have seen it in a student who gave up his childhood prejudices to become friends with a family of another race. I have seen it in a husband who gave up his cheery platitudes to join his wife in her trek toward death. I have seen it in a businessman who risked his career to protest his company's policy. Each put out the light that he had lived by, and each discovered that although there was darkness, there were also points of light that had never before been visible. There was a new creation.

For the student the new creation was finding his common humanity. For the husband it was the strength that flowed between him and his wife as he held her withering hand. For the businessman it was reclaiming the integrity that had been slipping from his grasp.

Each of these persons had possessed a general faith in Christ for some time, but not until they were pressed by their particular situations did they feel themselves to be part of the new creation. Christ's transforming power became for them more than religious Musak which the church plays to soothe our nerves while we sit in death's waiting room. They could feel Christ's creative power moving in and through them. It was the power of acceptance conquering prejudice. It was the power of shared sorrow crippling death's terror. It was the power of conscience challenging wrong. To know this power in our own lives is to be saved. It is to be "in Christ" and to be part of the new creation.

The experience of the student, the husband, and the businessman is like that of star watchers who consider the heavenly bodies beautiful yet light-years beyond their reach. As the watchers become more knowledgeable, they realize that their own bodies are made from elements of the same cataclysm that catapulted the nebulae into the far reaches of space. They feel a material solidarity with the universe. (See Carl Sagan and Jerome Agel, *The Cosmic Connection;* Doubleday & Co., 1973.)

In the same way, we often think of the new crea-

tion in Christ as a beautiful yet distant reality. It is
a preacher's phrase, the poetry of theology rather
than the prose of common life. Without denying
the grandeur of God, we need to grasp our Christo-
logical connection as fully as astronomers claim
humanity's cosmic connection. We are substan-
tively related to the glory we behold through the
telescopes of Scripture and tradition. The new creation is not light-years away. We are part of it. The
new creation moves in and through us. It is the
force that wells up in the heart and drives the
human mind to new knowledge, new insight, new
courage. It is the tide of strength that rises within
and enables us to endure those tragedies which at
first we thought we could never face. It is the dis-
satisfaction with things as they are and the struggle for a better order in our lives and in society.

The new creation is everywhere about us. Even
though

Generations have trod, have trod, have trod;
    And all is seared with trade; bleared, smeared with
        toil;
    And wears man's smudge and shares man's
        smell. . . .

. . . .
    There lives the dearest freshness deep down things;
And though the last lights off the black West went
    Oh, morning, at the brown brink eastward, springs—
Because the Holy Ghost over the bent
    World broods with warm breast and with ah! bright
        wings.
                    (Gerard Manley Hopkins, "God's Grandeur")

Many people see and smell the smear and the
smudge, but "the dearest freshness deep down
things" goes unnoticed. The dome of meaning that
arches over their lives is a suffocating cynicism,
while for the poet "the Holy Ghost over the bent

World broods with warm breast and with ah!
bright wings." To know that existence is spanned
by a warm and bright reality opens our eyes to "the
dearest freshness" around us.

The poet says this reality "broods" over us. From
the imagery of the "wings" and "breast" it is clear
that Hopkins is employing the metaphor of a
mother hen protecting her offspring. This is the
same image that Christ uses when he weeps over
the holy city: "O Jerusalem, Jerusalem, killing the
prophets and stoning those who are sent to you!
How often would I have gathered your children
together as a hen gathers her brood under her
wings, and you would not! Behold your house is
forsaken and desolate" (Matt. 23:37-38). Life is "forsaken and desolate" when the truth under which
we gather as a people is not the caring reality of
Christ. Life in Christ means life under Christ—
under his love, under his rule, under his protection.

HIDING BENEATH A PRIVATE HEAVEN

Because we live in an age of individualism most
people do not share a common dome of meaning
with the rest of humanity. People build their own
heaven. This is what the citizens of Jerusalem did.
As a result, they killed the prophets and stoned
those who were sent to them. Hovering under their
own religious interpretation of life, the people did
not recognize those who came from heaven, who
represented the just and loving truth of God. Their
artificial heavens had to collapse so they could live
under God's roof. Jesus put it this way: "Truly,
truly, I say to you, unless one is born from above, he
cannot see the kingdom of God" (John 3:3, margin).
We usually translate "from above" with the En-

glish word "anew," but the Greek adverb carries both meanings. To be "born from above" means to realize that we have built heaven from below. We have fashioned our understanding of life out of our own fears, hopes, expectations, experience. When we are born from above we accept the meaning and reality that are constructed by God rather than by ourselves. We step out of the planetarium of human purpose and look into the real sky of God's universe. The stars that guide us are no longer the values which we project, but the truth which God makes to shine. We live by God's acceptance instead of our prejudice, by God's mercy instead of our vengeance, by God's peace instead of our anxiety, by God's justice instead of our oppression.

To be born from above involves such a total reorientation in our lives that the idea at first baffles and threatens us. Nicodemus asks: "How can a man be born when he is old? Can he enter a second time into his mother's womb and be born?" (John 3:4). Nicodemus' question reflects more than a failure to understand Jesus. It issues from the fear that grabs us all when we are confronted with the possibility of losing our cozy world. We want to retreat to the womb. We want to return to the securest place we have ever known. Quite often we find it in an old-fashioned religion that has no critical awareness. We are willing to be "born again" but not "born from above." We are willing to reclaim the faith of a simpler age but not to confront the awesome demand that we give up every fake heaven, including a religious belief that has all the answers. This was Nicodemus' problem. He had that old-time religion. What he feared was the power that cannot be contained, the Spirit that "blows where it wills" (John 3:8).

Most of us, like Nicodemus, hide beneath a pri-

vate heaven. If it is not religious, then it is philo-
sophical or political or cultural. We too fear the
unexpected gust of truth that shall blow down the
house of cards in which we live.

Solid as a Rock, Uncontrollable as the Wind

The wind of the Spirit and the dome of meaning
are contrasting images. The one is airy, the other
solid. The one is unpredictable, the other fixed in
place. But faith makes them complementary
rather than conflicting. Only when we hold both of
them together do we understand the new creation
that has come through Christ.

When we are in Christ, there are some realities
of which we are absolutely certain. We know that
God's love is unconditional. God's grace is unfath-
omable. God's loyalty is unending. God's promise is
unbreakable. God's purpose is unconquerable.
There is to life and to all of existence a dependable
structure that can never be broken or wounded or
even slightly shaken. To use an image dear to
many psalmists: God is a rock.

When we are in Christ we also discover that God
moves in ways that our deepest faith could never
have imagined. God's love shows up in the most
surprising places. God's grace is shared with the
most unlikely strangers. God's loyalty endures our
disloyalty. God's promise comes true for us just
when we thought it was broken. God's purpose
makes sense to us when all human meaning breaks
down. There is to life and to all of existence an
essential dynamic that can never be predicted or
pigeonholed or even in the tiniest way controlled.
Reality is wide open: God is Spirit.

God the rock keeps us from being wishy-washy.

God the Spirit keeps us from being dogmatic. When we are in Christ, "the old creation has gone"—the floundering for faith, the constant attention to fads, the moral fuzziness. God the rock steadies us.

The "old creation" also includes the rigidity, the closed-mindedness, the uptightness of our former life. These too are gone when we are in Christ. God the Spirit opens us up.

"Behold, the new has come." Not a new religion. Not a new philosophy. Not a new program. But a new creation—a new way of living, a new way of being! We have seen it in Jesus Christ, who was deadly serious about "justice and mercy and faith" (Matt. 23:23) but who went to a lot of dinner parties and quaffed his drink and devoured his bread with such gusto that people called him "a glutton and a drunkard" (Luke 7:34). Sacred life with wine on the breath and crumbs in the beard; common life with grace in the heart and holy power in the body. This is the new creation that scared the religious establishment of Palestine. This is the new creation who still would gather us under his care as "a hen gathers her brood under her wings." This is the new creation who is our dome of meaning and our wind of life. To be part of this creation is to be saved.

Chapter 5

From Fear

Not everything was gray. Rust-colored marigolds stood in a drinking glass on a chipped enamel table, and the calendar of "This Week's Activities" was bordered with red construction paper. But these colors were only whispers in the two-toned drab of institutional walls.

"State Department of Mental Hygiene" was stitched over the breast pocket of the attendant's gown.

"Step in here, please, and I'll get your brother in a minute."

Alex walked into a cubbyhole of a room. Flowered curtains with pressed-in wrinkles hung over the window like bedspreads on a clothesline. Alex waited thirty seconds. Or since the world was created. The door opened and Mark drifted in. Drifted, not walked. His body never moved with the clear action of lifting one foot in front of the other.

"Hello, Mark, I've come to visit you."

"Who are you?" The voice was the same color as the walls, and there were no marigolds in the eyes.

"Why, Mark! I'm your brother Alex."

"No, you aren't. I know who you are. I saw your ship. I saw it last night in the sky. You're going to get me because I failed the movement."

"Mark, that's nonsense. I'm Alex. Your brother Alex."

"No, you're not. You're just disguised. You're all disguised. You look like my family, but you're not my family. I know this letter is from the kingdom. You cannot fool me."

"What letter?"

"This letter that pretends to come from Mom." Mark brought out a letter written in their mother's usual combination of print and cursive.

"That's Mom's hand, Mark. Look, that's just the way she starts her sentences: the first word printed and the rest in longhand. We used to joke about it. Remember?"

"It's all part of your plot. I saw your ship. I saw it last night in the sky."

That is as much of the setting and the conversation as Alex could tell me before he sat down and wept.

"It was as though I were not even talking with my brother Mark. He seemed to be possessed. Some other person, some demon inside him had taken control of his brain."

Alex was a research chemist. He was a man of science whose world was qualitative analysis and the periodic chart of elements. When he had first heard of Mark's psychosis he understood it as a problem of chemical imbalance. But when he witnessed its personal effects upon his brother, he reached beyond a physiological explanation to the language of spiritual possession. Alex was not abandoning his scientific understanding; he was only expressing a dimension of his experience that could never be captured in the most perfect chemical analysis of his brother's problems. There was no formula to describe what Alex felt when Mark said: "You're all disguised. You look like my family,

but you're not my family." To hear those words
from the mouth of the same brother with whom he
had wrestled, fished, sailed, skied, and grown up
was to encounter a demon. It was to come face-to-
face with the power of chaos that can blow to
smithereens what is good and true and precious in
our lives.

JESUS AND THE DEMONS

The same power that possessed Alex' brother
Mark confronted Jesus at the beginning of his ministry. Jesus had been teaching in the synagogue at
Capernaum. The congregation had listened intensely because his words carried a weight and a
conviction that the authorities lacked. He had just
finished speaking when "there was in their synagogue a man with an unclean spirit; and he cried
out, 'What have you to do with us, Jesus of
Nazareth? Have you come to destroy us? I know
who you are, the Holy One of God' " (Mark 1:23).
How awkward for the congregation. It was a holy
moment. They were reflecting on the truth of what
they had heard, and now the town idiot broke the
spell with his blather. That madman! Who let him
in? Why wasn't he chained up as they did in other
communities? (See Mark 5:4.) And the drivel he
uttered: "the Holy One of God." Yes, the young
preacher was good, but not even a gifted rabbi de-
served such extravagant praise.
    Before anyone could lead the fool out, Jesus took
control of the situation: " 'Be silent, and come out
of him!' And the unclean spirit, convulsing him
and crying with a loud voice, came out of him"
(Mark 1:25-26). Embarrassment turned to awe.
What was going on here? Not only does this fellow

from Nazareth speak with authority, but "he commands even the unclean spirits, and they obey him" (Mark 1:27). It was a scene that was to be replayed throughout Jesus' ministry. In the country of the Gerasenes he drove the unclean spirits out of a man who lived in a graveyard (Mark 5:1ff.). In the region of Tyre and Sidon he cast the demon out of a Greek woman's daughter (Mark 7:24). And after the transfiguration, he freed an epileptic boy from the spirit that sent him into convulsions (Mark 9:14ff.). There were numerous other occasions, not all described in detail, but summarized by the Gospel of Mark: "Whenever the unclean spirits beheld him, they fell down before him and cried out, 'You are the Son of God'" (Mark 3:11). The demons identified Jesus more readily than the crowds or the disciples because he represented the power antithetically opposed to them. He embodied that force through which "all things hold together" (Col. 1:17), while they were the forces that seek to drive everything apart.

If the demons did not recognize who Jesus was, then existence would be absurd. It would mean that there is no clear distinction between the power for order and sanity and the power for chaos and madness. The vertebrae of existence would dissolve and life would be a colloid, as indefinable in shape as the ooze of an amoeba. The birth certificates that showed Alex and Mark to be brothers could claim no more objective truth than Mark's belief that his family was a host of enemies from outer space disguised to get him.

The gospel affirms that madness is not the essential nature of life. There is a greater power for wholeness that can restore the aberrant self. Jesus had this power to such a degree that "he cast out

the spirits with a word" (Matt. 8:16). With a word!
If we are not to reduce Jesus to a witch doctor and
his exorcism to hocus-pocus, then we must understand the nature of that word.

EXORCISM AND CREATION

For the Gospel writers, a word from Jesus is
more than the incantation of a shaman. It represents the same power that in the beginning said,
" 'Let there be light'; and there was light" (Gen.
1:3). Because Christ himself is the Word through
whom "all things were made," his spoken words in
the New Testament share in that authority which
brought the world into existence. Jesus' exorcisms
represent more than psychological healing; they
are the reenactment of the primordial cosmic act
by which God first subdued the forces of chaos.

"The earth was without form and void, and darkness was upon the face of the deep; and the Spirit
of God was moving over the face of the waters"
(Gen. 1:2). The Hebrew word for "deep" here comes
from the name of a chaos monster, Tiamat, who
appears in Babylonian mythology. The writers of
Genesis, ch. 1, have torn the fangs from the monster by reducing him from a personalized force to
a vaguer concept, "the deep." But not all of the Old
Testament depersonalizes the power of chaos.
There are a number of passages where chaos takes
the form of a beast, known variously as Leviathan
(Job 41:1; Ps. 104:26), the serpent (Isa. 27:1), the dragon (Isa. 51:9), and Rahab (Ps. 89:10). Salvation
means victory over this monster: "Yet God my King
is from of old, working salvation in the midst of the
earth. Thou didst divide the sea by thy might; thou
didst break the heads of the dragons on the waters.

Thou didst crush the heads of Leviathan, thou didst give him as food for the creatures of the wilderness" (Ps. 74:12-14). Salvation is an act of cosmic exorcism. Just as Jesus drove demons out of individuals, so God already had conquered the demonic forces that were present in creation.

Cosmic and personal exorcism are interrelated. The cosmic is the precondition of the personal, and the personal is a witness to the reality of the cosmic.

Jesus was able to move into the center of people's personalities and free them from evil spirits because he embodied the very power that had already subdued these forces "in the midst of the earth." The wholeness that Jesus restored to persons was an extension of the wholeness that God had brought to the universe. For Jesus, psychology is rooted in cosmology. That is why he tells the healed demoniac of the Gerasenes, "Return to your home, and declare how much God has done for you" (Luke 8:39). Jesus' exorcism is not some bizarre spiritualist phenomenon. It is a witness to God. The exorcism is evidence that the power for wholeness and sanity is greater than the power for chaos and madness.

Jesus sends the former demoniac home. The man's return symbolizes his complete restoration. Not only is his psyche back in order but also his relationship to his family and society.

Jesus commissions the man to interpret his personal healing as a sign of God's saving activity: "Declare how much God has done for you." Jesus wants the world to know that the same God who did "crush the heads of Leviathan" is still driving out the beasts that tear the human self asunder. We are not abandoned to fight alone those forces which take possession of people's minds. There is a power

who is on the side of our healthiest selves and who
since creation has been subduing the dynamics of
insanity wherever they have been.

When we step into the two-toned drab of the
state hospital and our brother says: "You're all disguised. You look like my family, but you're not my
family," then we need to know that the power
which worked through Jesus is still moving among
us. It is not a matter of choosing between religious
faith and modern medicine. We have already seen
how such a simplistic dichotomy breaks down in
the face of experience. Alex the chemist needed
both a scientific and a spiritual understanding in
order to comprehend the magnitude of his
brother's problem. The two are in no way opposed.
Faith celebrates the restoration of a human being's
sanity in whatever way it is accomplished. Drugs,
therapy groups, personal counseling, prayer, faith,
the concern of family and friends—all of these can
be extensions of the same exorcising power that
"[broke] the heads of the dragons on the waters"
and that brought peace to the Gerasene demoniac.

"And those who had seen it told them [the other
Gerasenes] how he who had been possessed with
demons was healed" (Luke 8:36). The Greek word
that is translated "healed" is the word for "saved."
Salvation to those herdsmen who had witnessed
Jesus' power meant this: "A man who once we
bound with chains and kept under guard (v. 29)
because of his ranting has returned to his right
mind and to his community." Salvation is conquering the forces that disintegrate human personality.
Salvation is any therapeutic process that restores
people to themselves and to society.

For Alex' brother Mark, who was eventually dis-
charged from the hospital, salvation was leaving

behind the marigolds on the chipped enamel table and returning to his garden at home. Salvation was forgetting about the calendar of "This Week's Activities" trimmed in red construction paper and making a date for the movies with an old friend who was glad to have him back. Salvation was coming home and reading the shopping list on the refrigerator and noticing how his mother still printed the first word and then used cursive. Salvation was looking at his family and seeing not enemies from outer space but persons who loved him. Salvation was knowing that Christ had cast the demons out of him.

TWO KINGDOMS

"Then all the people of the surrounding country of the Gerasenes asked him to depart from them; for they were seized with great fear" (Luke 8:37). Salvation as exorcism is scary stuff. The observation of madness in others disturbs the demons within ourselves. And the healing of madness leaves a feeling that something awesome has happened. This intuition is evidence of the cosmological battle that lies beneath the psychological struggle. Like the Gerasenes, we are seized with great fear because there has been a confrontation between darkness and light, madness and sanity, hell and heaven. There has been a battle between two kingdoms which are usually hidden from sight but whose powers we now have observed, first in the madness and now in the healing. Our fear stems from the enormity of forces that lie beyond our control and comprehension. The fear is awakened by the exorcism as much as it is by the demons. Can

anything powerful enough to take on demons be
trusted in itself? And what about the future? For
the present there is peace, but what force shall tri-
umph in the end?

Jesus' opponents knew about this fear. In an attempt to discredit him they suggested that his
power of exorcism was another manifestation of
the demonic spirit. Jesus countered them by point-
ing out the absurdity of their position: "How can
Satan cast out Satan? If a kingdom is divided
against itself, that kingdom cannot stand. And if a
house is divided against itself, that house will not
be able to stand. And if Satan has risen up against
himself and is divided, he cannot stand, but is coming to an end" (Mark 3:23-26).

Jesus sees life divided between two realms: the
kingdom of Satan and the Kingdom of God. They
represent the polarities of existence: Anarchy versus structure. Madness versus sanity. Fragmenta-
tion versus wholeness. Demons versus the Spirit. It
is against the order of reality for either kingdom to
be at odds with itself. If evil were tossing out evil,
then evil would self-destruct, and Jesus is too much
of a realist to believe that. He knows that great
strength is required to overcome the demonic
power that torments the possessed: "But no one can
enter a strong man's house and plunder his goods,
unless he first binds the strong man; then indeed he
may plunder his house" (Mark 3:27). Jesus' violent
imagery implies that Satan is the homeowner of
existence and that Christ is a thief! Salvation is an
act of breaking and entering. The image is a tour
de force parable in which Jesus simultaneously describes the interior, subjective experience of the
individual being healed and the exterior, transcen-
dent perspective of God.

For the disturbed person the attempt to bring

him or her back to reality is nothing less than an
attack on the world that person already occupies. It
appears that the doctor, the counselor, the attendant, the chaplain, the family are all plundering the
patient's psychic home. In the Gospels this is sym-
bolized by the questions and pleas that the evil
spirits make to Jesus: "What have you to do with us,
Jesus of Nazareth? Have you come to destroy us?"
(Mark 1:24). "What have you to do with me, Jesus,
Son of the Most High God? I adjure you by God, do
not torment me" (Mark 5:7).

Exorcism for God is breaking into the house that
is hostile to the divine presence. God is locked out
because the demonic force has bolted the door. But
God's power is greater than any power that would
keep God out. God breaks the lock on our mad
world, ties up the demonic master of the household, and steals our insanity from us.

The significance of the parable extends beyond
exorcism to what the healing represents: the coming of the Kingdom of God. The Gospel parallels of
Matthew and Luke make this meaning explicit,
"But if it is by the Spirit of God that I cast out
demons, the kingdom of God has come upon you"
(Matt. 12:28, cf. Luke 11:20). The exorcisms of the
possessed show that God is taking over as the
homeowner of existence. The healing of demo-
niacs is only the most dramatic and visible expression of a process that permeates reality.

To recognize the pervasive character of God's
exorcising activity is to see that even the sanest of
us are possessed and need to be plundered by God.
There are fears, anxieties, compulsions, hatreds,
and prejudices that hold us in bondage. We would
like to be rational people and throw out these demonic forces but find that we cannot do it on our
own. John Donne put it to God this way:

I, like an usurpt towne, to'another due,
Labour to'admit you, but Oh, to no end;
Reason, your viceroy in mee, mee should defend,
But is captiv'd, and proves weake or untrue.

(from Holy Sonnet XIV)

Even reason, supposedly God's deputy ruler or "viceroy," is controlled by unreasonable powers. As individuals we say that the reasonable thing would be to forget and forgive, but our need for vengeance is welded to our memory. As a country we know that expanding our nuclear overkill will not make us any more secure, yet we continue to build our arsenal. Our sane world is as mad as any asylum, only the inmates are nations instead of individuals. Salvation is the divine theft of our madness—be it the psychodynamic disturbance of the self or the military lunacy of international politics.

In the Bible people believe that God has the power to relieve both kinds of insanity. Isaiah pictures the deliverance of Israel as a victory over the demonic forces that have threatened the nation's existence: "In that day the Lord with his hard and great and strong sword will punish Leviathan, the fleeing serpent, Leviathan the twisting serpent, and he will slay the dragon that is in the sea" (Isa. 27:1). And at a much more personal level the Syrophoenician woman falls at Jesus' feet and begs him to cast out the demon that torments her daughter (Mark 7:24ff.). Together the two stories signify the comprehensiveness of God's exorcising activity. Isaiah's vision proclaims that God does not heal possessed individuals only to leave them in a mad world. The story of the Syrophoenician woman's daughter reminds us that God is not restoring the world only to leave it in the hands of disturbed people. God is exorcising both nations and individuals, both history and personality, both the cosmos and the self.

The totality of God's activity judges the ridiculous arguments that often rage in the church about whether to save individuals or structures. God is working on both. If we would be aligned with God's restoring purpose, then we must do the same.

I recall a middle-class white woman who tutored a black woman for her high school equivalency diploma. The woman not only passed with high grades but went on to get a professional degree. A political activist friend once questioned the value of the tutor's efforts because they were aimed only at an individual and did not change "the system"—the imbroglio of cultural, economic, and educational prejudice that keeps black people from realizing their potential. The tutoring exorcised the demon of self-doubt that had haunted the black woman, but it did not cast out the evil spirit of racism that thrives in the system. The Biblically informed response to this situation is to celebrate the exorcism that did take place and to work for the same healing in the larger structures of society.

Salvation is the look of self-esteem that shone in the black woman's face when she received her degree. Salvation is also the board of education's acting to transform "equal opportunity for all" from slogan into policy. In each case the Kingdom of God has come upon us because demons have been cast out. God exorcises both the psyche and society.

THE ULTIMATE EXORCISM

No door shuts with a more terrifying sound than the door that leads to the ward with the flowered

curtains hung like bedspreads on a clothesline.
Confrontation with the demonic is always devastating. We are like the man whose possessed son
Jesus' disciples could not heal. The man appeals to
Jesus himself but acknowledges: "I believe; help
my unbelief!" (Mark 9:24). In the face of the demonic we are all a mixture of belief and unbelief.

We are like Alex, the chemist and brother of
Mark. Whenever Alex with tears in his eyes drove
his brother back to the state hospital, when he
drank stale coffee from the vending machines and
waited for the admitting doctor to arrive, when he
signed the forms filled with diagnostic terms, he
believed but didn't believe. Alex believed that
there was hope. He believed that the routine and
the supervision would bring Mark back to the family once more. He believed that when he took Mark
a carton of cigarettes the next week, he would already be improving.

Alex believed, but how he wanted help with his
unbelief! Unbelief in the treatment. Unbelief in the
hospital. Unbelief in his brother's recovery. Unbelief in God.

Our mixture of belief and unbelief reflects more
than a psychological state. It is rooted in the nature
of reality: the kingdoms of the demonic and of God
which Jesus saw locked in battle with each other.
Our confused feelings witness to the truth of Jesus'
vision. We would not believe so strongly in the possibility of emotional healing if it were not that
some power for human wholeness has penetrated
to the innermost being of our selves. Likewise, we
would not be so disturbed by doubt if it were not
that an opposing reality has also invaded the center of our existence.

Because our struggle involves something more

than psychological dynamics only a truth greater than our subjective state can bring peace. The book of Revelation pictures this truth as a battle in which the demonic forces—represented by the beast, the false prophet, and the devil—are "thrown into the lake of fire and sulphur, . . . for ever and ever" (Rev. 20:10). Since the scene takes place beyond history, it does not suggest that our inner struggle between belief and unbelief is resolved in this life. Rather, our belief in the ultimate exorcism of existence empowers us to face the doubts and the demons that confront us without giving in to despair. Martin Luther captured the tension of conflict and confidence that marks the inner state of the believer:

> And though this world, with devils filled,
> Should threaten to undo us,
> We will not fear, for God has willed
> His truth to triumph through us.
> The prince of darkness grim,
> We tremble not for him;
> His rage we can endure,
> For lo! his doom is sure,
> One little word shall fell him.
> ("A Mighty Fortress Is Our God,"
> stanza 3)

One little word! Luther returns us to him who "cast out the spirits with a word" (Matt. 8:16). Salvation is knowing that Jesus Christ is the ultimate victor. Salvation is hugging our brother before he enters the ward painted in two-toned drab and knowing that someday in a way beyond our knowledge, beyond our drugs, beyond our pain, beyond our separation, beyond our tears a word shall destroy those forces which now tear us apart. Christ shall speak and the demons shall be vanquished "for ever and

ever." Because of this ultimate exorcism "we tremble not" for the prince of darkness. "His rage we
can endure." The door to the ward shuts. But we
can endure. We can endure! This is salvation.

Chapter 6

From Smugness

"Of course Mrs. Grantly forgave Mrs. Proudie all her offences, and wished her well, and was at peace with her, in the Christian sense of the word, as with all other women. But under this forbearance and meekness, and perhaps, we may say, wholly unconnected with it, there was certainly a current of antagonistic feeling which, in the ordinary unconsidered language of every day, men and women do call hatred" (Anthony Trollope, *Framley Parsonage,* p. 161; Harcourt, Brace and World, 1962).

Forgiving yet hating! We all know the contradiction. We felt it when we were children. Our parents made us shake hands and accept our friend's apology, but all the time we were plotting how we would get even. We feel the tension as adults when we try to forget how someone has wronged us. Long after we have said, "I forgive you," the sting of our wound persists. We keep rubbing it as though it were a physical scar and recalling how it was inflicted. Each time we touch the sore we conjure up its initial pain. Oh, but nobody knows how we suffered!

Vengeance has a delectable sweetness, but we pay a terrible price for feasting on this fruit. It clogs love's arteries with self-righteousness and reduces our interpersonal relationships to a legal contest in which we keep track of every wrong.

How to Bury the Hatchet

Forgiveness does not issue from moral obliga-tion. It requires something stronger than a sense of duty to break through our bitterness. If we forgive because we *ought* to, we will be like Mrs. Grantly. The novelist pictures her as a "Christian lady" who is at peace with her opponent "in the Christian sense of the word." Like many believers, Mrs. Grantly transforms the spontaneous, heartfelt character of grace into a formal, rigid legalism. "Of course Mrs. Grantly forgave Mrs. Proudie." Of course! Because social convention demanded it. Be-cause she knew it was proper and fitting. Because from the time she was a child the church told her it was what God commanded. Because it was the Christian thing to do.

Jesus struggled with this problem throughout his ministry: how to nurture forgiveness in peo-ple's lives without turning it into law and destroy-ing its essential nature. Jesus kept bumping into the Mrs. Grantly mentality.

Simon the Pharisee (Luke 7:36-50) was a Mrs. Grantly. Just as the lady prided herself on her ec-clesiastical status—her husband was an archdea-con—so Simon was keenly aware of his religious distinction. Just as Mrs. Grantly relished the eve-ning parties of the London socialites, so Simon was willing to enliven his own soiree with the contro-versial rabbi from Nazareth. And Simon, like Mrs. Grantly, was comfortable with the formal require-ments of religion but disturbed by the humble human dress of God's forgiveness: "And behold, a

woman of the city, who was a sinner, when she
learned that [Jesus] was at table in the Pharisee's
house brought an alabaster flask of ointment, and
standing behind him at his feet, weeping, she
began to wet his feet with her tears, and wiped
them with the hair of her head, and kissed his feet,
and anointed them with the ointment. Now when
the Pharisee who had invited him saw it, he said to
himself, 'If this man were a prophet, he would
have known who and what sort of woman this is
who is touching him, for she is a sinner.' "

Simon speaks only to himself, because he, like
Mrs. Grantly, is a master of what is proper and
fitting. It is awkward enough that a woman of ques-
tionable morals has barged in on his party and that
a supposedly holy man has lacked the presence of
mind to stop her display of affection. Better to keep
silent and not grant any dignity to the scene by
calling attention to it.

Jesus reads the mind of his host and interrupts
his reveries of righteousness. " 'Simon, I have
something to say to you.' And he answered, 'What
is it, Teacher?' 'A certain creditor had two debtors;
one owed five hundred denarii, and the other fifty.
When they could not pay, he forgave them both.
Now which of them will love him more?' "

Simon gives a tentative response: "The one, I
suppose, to whom he forgave more." As cool as Mrs.
Grantly at one of Mrs. Proudie's parties, Simon
tries to keep his distance from Jesus' parable. For
a brief moment Jesus leaves the subject at an abstract level: "You have judged rightly."

Then throwing propriety to the winds, Jesus
drives forward with heavenly grace: "Do you see
this woman?" Simon has been seeing her all evening and hoping that she would disappear. He has
been seeing her and thinking how awful she is and

how good he is. He has been seeing her and wondering whatever possessed him to invite this Jesus in the first place and how he will save face with his other guests. And now Jesus says: "Do you see this woman? I entered your house, you gave me no water for my feet, but she has wet my feet with her tears and wiped them with her hair. You gave me no kiss, but from the time I came in she has not ceased to kiss my feet. You did not anoint my head with oil, but she has anointed my feet with ointment."

The contrasts that Jesus draws between Simon's and the woman's hospitality are an extension of his parable. The tears, the ointment, the touch of hands and hair are all expressions of the love that is freed through forgiveness. Even though the declaration of pardon—"Your sins are forgiven"—does not come until after the woman's actions, it is clear that her affection toward Jesus flows out of a sure sense of his forgiveness and acceptance. Like the debtor freed from his bill of five hundred denarii, the woman has been forgiven much and so she loves much. Hers is not a spiritualized love but the outpouring of the heart that moves through the body with sensual strength.

Salvation is the ecstasy of being genuinely pardoned. Salvation is being so happy that we kiss the person who has forgiven us. Salvation is buying an extravagant gift—for the woman it was ointment— and presenting it with tears and embraces to the person who has taken us back. It is not a matter of making up for the past, because the past is over. It is not a matter of buying our way to acceptance, because we are already accepted. It is not a promise that we will never fail again, because our pardon has not changed us into God. Our gift represents the irrepressible joy of knowing that we are forgiven. Truly forgiven. Not forgiven and hated.

But forgiven and loved! Forgiven and accepted.
Forgiven and freed. We sleep again. We tell the old
jokes again, and once more our shared laughter
rings like music. The glory that had passed from
the earth returns. Heaven smiles, and we remember to pick up butter and eggs from the store on the
way home, because we are not preoccupied with
guilt. This is forgiveness. This is salvation.

THE DEVIL'S MOST DEVIOUS DISGUISE

"Your faith has saved you: go in peace" (Luke
7:50). These are Jesus' last words to the woman at
Simon's house. What has she been saved from? The
most obvious answer is: from her sins. But Jesus'
benediction may have another meaning. He has
already declared the woman's sins forgiven (v. 48),
so that in these parting words he may be referring
to something besides her pardon. The woman has
been saved from becoming like Simon the Pharisee! She has been saved from turning into a Mrs.
Grantly! The woman's openness to Jesus' forgiveness has kept her from becoming formal, rigid, le-
galistic, and unloving.
    When we say salvation is forgiveness, we mean
two things: the act of pardon and the receptivity to
forgiveness. Without the second of these, the first
holds no personal meaning. This is Simon's problem. Not that he is an evil man, but that he is a good
man and knows it. Simon has been seduced by the
devil wearing his most devious disguise. That disguise is nothing less than the perfectionism of the
religious person, the feeling that we do not need to
be forgiven because we are already good people.
We always make four dozen chocolate chip cookies
for the church bake sale. We take in the Rotary

exchange students. We belong to the booster club
for school athletics. We attend Sunday worship
regularly (unless the sailing or the skiing is too
good to miss). We pay our taxes, and we never riot
or break the law (except for letting the speed creep
above fifty-five on the expressway). We try always
to do right (though now and then we do something
wrong and need forgiveness). We are upstanding
citizens. So was Simon.

Simon considered himself a higher class of
being than the woman. She was beneath his level.
He did not recognize the common humanity that
he shared with her; he did not feel that he needed
God's forgiveness as much as she did. Yet this is
precisely the awareness that could save him, save
him from his haughtiness and save him from his
inability to love with abandon.

Salvation is realizing that no matter how good
we have been, our debt to God is more than pocket
change. We have defaulted on the divine investment in humanity. God has poured love, acceptance, and forgiveness into us, and we have lived as
though we were bankrupt. We have not been the
forgiving, loving people that God has empowered
us to be. Still God pardons us. God erases the debt
and day by day replenishes heaven's account on
earth with vast sums of love and grace.

MISERS OR SPENDTHRIFTS

The woman at Simon's house was a spendthrift.
She responded to Christ's forgiveness with extravagant warmth. Many people are more miserly.
They stash away God's riches in the vaults of their
own heart. Being forgiven does not transform them
into forgiving people.

Jesus was familiar with this quirk of the human personality. He told a parable about a king's servant who refuses to grant someone an extension on his debt, even though the king has just canceled an enormous sum which the servant owed (Matt. 18: 23-35). The servant wants forgiveness for himself and the full requirement of the law for his debtor. The king flies into a rage, takes back his pardon, and throws the unforgiving servant into jail. "So also my heavenly Father will do to every one of you, if you do not forgive your brother from your heart."

Jesus' severe words seem to reduce forgiveness to the very thing which we earlier claimed it cannot be: a matter of moral obligation. "Thou shalt forgive" appears to be the eleventh commandment. Such a reading of the parable, however, neglects the loving character of the king who earlier in the story forgives the servant his entire debt. The king is furious because he takes forgiveness seriously. If the king went his merry way when he discovered the servant's unrelenting demand for payment, then the king's act of pardon would appear as whim rather than policy. Sometimes he would be interested in forgiveness and sometimes not. It would all depend on his mood. The king would be a tyrant. His subjects would never know whether they were to lose their heads or have a place at the palace table.

But the king does get angry. He is upset that the servant did not extend to another debtor the same forgiveness he had received. The king's outrage proves the genuiness of his pardon.

Jesus' parable and warning make explicit the implications of God's graciousness. The command to forgive is not a moral decree delivered out of the blue. The command tells us to implement the forgiveness which we already have experienced: "As

the Lord has forgiven you, so you also must forgive" (Col. 3:13). The rule flows out of the reality.
Heaven's law is based on heaven's grace. "It's all
right. I forgive you. We're still friends." These
words are the fulfillment of a commandment, but
a commandment that makes sense to us because
we ourselves have been forgiven. Like the children
of loving parents, we understand the command to
love because we have been loved.

IN PURSUIT OF PARDON

"So if you are offering your gift at the altar, and
there remember that your brother has something
against you, leave your gift there before the altar
and go; first be reconciled to your brother, and then
come and offer your gift" (Matt. 5:23-24).

Read the text closely. It does *not* say, "If you
remember something that you have against your
brother," but rather, if your brother "has something against you." You may feel completely at
peace with your brother. You may be sitting in
church thinking the warmest thoughts about ev-
erybody in the world. You may love all people with
a deep, sincere, and godly love. But Jesus wants to
know: Is there someone outside the sanctuary who
despite your good feelings has something against
you? If there is, don't even stay for the invocation
and the first hymn. Get out of that pew, and don't
worry about making it back in time for the offer-
tory or even the benediction.

Knock on your neighbor's door.

Or call up your co-worker.

Or take your child down to the diner and order
some pancakes.

But whatever you do, have it out with the person

who is angry with you. Find out why the mood. Why the hostile look. Why the constant negativism. What happened? What went wrong? What did you do or say? For the love of Christ (literally!) be reconciled to your brother or your sister. If you have to ask for forgiveness, ask.

Then, when you have shaken hands and your friend feels as warmly about you as you were feeling in the sanctuary, return to the church. If the congregation has gone home, slip into a pew and offer a prayer of thanks because God has just saved you. Saved you from religious smugness. Saved you from a broken relationship.

After your prayer, put your offering in the treasurer's box in the church office. Don't worry that you missed church. Next week when you hear the gospel it will sound like thunder in your heart, and you may weep.

Christ's command to leave our gift at the altar and seek out our alienated neighbor is based on God's own action. We did not seek out God's pardon. God pursued us. We would gladly have stewed in our anger and our sin. But in Jesus Christ, God came after us. God left behind heaven's worship service in order to still earth's warfare. And that is why we can put down the Sunday bulletin, walk by the surprised ushers in the narthex, and finally get straightened out whatever has been wrong between us and our neighbor.

Not that this is an easy thing to do. It isn't. Our palms sweat and there is a knot in our stomach when we first approach our estranged friend. We may have felt fine back in church, but now that we have rung the doorbell and hear the footsteps in the front hall, we are filled with memories: The whispers of gossip which once we spoke aloud. A cheap trick. The unintended arrogance. The abuse of a confidence. The theft of an idea. Other dark rumblings. As the latch turns, we feel like Jacob returning to face the music with Esau: "Deliver me, I pray thee, from the hand of my brother, from the hand of Esau, for I fear him" (Gen. 32:11).

First a look of disbelief on the other side of the door. Then an extended hand, and before we can finish saying, "I came because I wanted to talk about . . . ," we know that our presence is understood. Again Jacob's words fill our heart if not our speech: "Truly to see your face is like seeing the face of God, with such favor have you received me" (Gen. 33:10). This is salvation. Not standing on the steps to the chancel, but standing on the front stoop of our neighbor's house and hearing the words: "Come on in. I'm so glad you're here. I know we've needed to talk for some time."

The minister's weekly declaration of pardon—"I tell you in the name of Jesus Christ you are forgiven"—becomes as real as the hot, black coffee our friend pours for us. We can taste the pardon. We can feel its warmth. The air is thick with God's rich brew of grace.

At the kitchen table spread with the Sunday cartoons and yesterday's ball scores and with our friend sitting across from us, the trumpet sounds. Heaven opens. We have left the altar to come to the throne of grace. For seeing our friend smile at us again is truly like seeing the face of God.

We dilute the second cup of coffee with sugar and cream.

Our friend chuckles. "You still don't know how to drink the stuff."

We are saved.

Chapter 7

From Sickness

Jesus was on the run. The woman could tell from his stride that he was headed someplace urgent. She was certain that it was he. She had never seen him before, but she had heard reports of what he could do. The crowd that followed him confirmed her impression.

Twelve years of illness passed through the woman's mind. A trickle of blood. At first she had hardly noticed it. But then it had persisted, persisted like the dribble from the side of an old wineskin. No matter how often the red streak was wiped away, it returned out of some tiny break in the membrane hidden from touch and sight.

The blood had stained more than her clothes. It had marked her heart with despair. The zealous keepers of the old religious law had seen to that. Although as a woman she was not supposed to study the sacred writings, one verse she knew well: "If a woman has a discharge of blood for many days, not at the time of her impurity, or if she has a discharge beyond the time of her impurity, all the days of the discharge she shall continue in uncleanness; as in the days of her impurity, she shall be unclean" (Lev. 15:25).

Unclean. Unclean! Unclean!! The woman felt it like the wrath of God every time she changed her

clothes and every time people kept their distance
from her. They viewed her as sin personified while
all the time she was just a bleeding person—bleeding in body and bleeding in soul.

The woman had hoped that the doctors could do
something. She had tried them all. Every time it
had been the same experience. Perhaps for a day or
even a week or two the blood had stopped. But she
would wake up one morning and feel again the
cursed damp. Then it would be off to the next phy-
sician.

Now she was financially broke and spiritually
broken. She dragged her body along the back
streets and alleys, looking with envy at the healthy
and with bitterness at the sanctimonious. They
thought themselves so holy because they did not
bleed. What would happen if she cut them with a
knife? Would springwater pour out?

But when the woman saw Jesus, the old hope
stirred again. All she had heard were reports: How
he cured a woman of her fever. How he cleansed a
leper. How he made a paralytic walk. It was only
hearsay picked up around the corner, and yet there
was the crowd pressing around him. How foolish
for the woman to believe and be disappointed once
more. How wretched to trust and have her trust
betrayed again. Yet she could not help herself.
Something rose inside her as powerful as the frost
that heaves the road and that cannot be paved over.

She would approach Jesus from behind. She
would not call to him or even reach for his body but
just for his robe and nothing more. She said to herself, "If I touch even his garments, I shall be made
well" (Mark 5:28). "Made well." The word that the
woman used was the word for "saved." She could
have used another, but what she was after was

nothing less than salvation. It would be salvation to wake up dry and clean.

Hope poured through her weakened body. She could see where the sweat had soaked through his robe between his shoulder blades. He was damp, too, as she was. He would share whatever power he had to heal her. She knew he would. She was convinced. She believed in him. She reached toward him. Forefinger almost there. A slight lean from the waist and the feel of cloth against the palm. "And immediately the hemorrhage ceased; and she felt in her body that she was healed of her disease" (Mark 5:29).

Touched. Stopped. Healed. The same certain feeling of having a deeply embedded splinter removed and saying, "There! that got it." A moment ago the blood had been running hard. It usually did when the woman moved vigorously. But now there was nothing. Not the scantest dribble. She was ready to slip away and wash and put on her cleanest garment and to thank God and thank God and thank God.

But even as she withdrew her hand, Jesus stopped and turned around. "Who touched my garments?" Jesus had felt power flowing out of him. Like anyone who has healed someone, Jesus was aware of the energy it draws from us to make another person whole. We feel the loss in more than the physical activity of nursing. We feel it in the depths of who we are, the current of power that flows from within us toward any person who trustingly turns to us for help: the child who is struggling with the flu, the sick elderly parent, the neighbor with a wounded marriage. After dealing with them we say, "We are drained."

Jesus felt the drain. Not even his closest friends

could convince him otherwise with their observation: "You see the crowd pressing around you, and
yet you say, 'Who touched me?' " (Mark 5:31).

There was a difference between the press of the
crowd and the touch of the woman. It is the difference between curiosity about Jesus and faith in
Jesus. The one is general; the other focused. The
one looks at Jesus with fascination; the other
reaches out to Jesus in hope.

"But the woman, knowing what had been done to
her, came in fear and trembling and fell down before him, and told him the whole truth" (Mark 5:
33). The "fear and trembling" may in part have
been her uncertainty about making a public scene,
the embarrassment of the crowd, and the way she
had come up behind Jesus. But the very phrase
"fear and trembling" usually has a deeper meaning. It is the way people react to the presence of the
Holy. In the Old Testament the earth "trembles" at
God's approach. The psalmist warns kings: "Serve
the Lord with fear, with trembling kiss his feet"
(Ps. 2:11-12). Paul reminds the Corinthians of how
they received the messengers of the gospel with
"fear and trembling" (I Cor. 2:3 and II Cor. 7:15).

The woman knew that Holy power had flowed
from Jesus to her. This was no magic force available to anyone who would handle Jesus' clothing. It
was and is the power that flows through trust,
through faith, through belief. Jesus is the supreme
bearer of this power, yet we feel it in other human
ways whenever we entrust ourselves to the healing
touch of someone else. We receive this power from
the hands of the surgeon. We receive it from the
neighbor who listens to our hurt and worry. We
receive it from the nurse who changes our dressing. We receive it from the person who loves us and
ends our rotten day with a kiss and a hug. It is a

power for physical healing; it is a power for psychological healing. It is one power that restores both body and psyche, that stops both bleeding flesh and bleeding heart.

BONES AND SOUL

To be healed is to be saved. We may not talk about our recovery in religious terms. We may not describe our inner state as one of "fear and trembling," yet we are close to the truth of these Biblical words whenever we are restored to health and find ourselves thinking: I can hardly believe it. I'm actually better. The wonder, the sense of a new lease on life, the gratitude that we feel toward people who helped us and toward friends and family who suffered with us—all witness that healing is something more than a purely physiological event.

I recall patients who told me where, how, and why their surgeon had operated. Sometimes they drew a picture of the procedure or showed one the doctor had sketched. Others recited the reasons and regimen of a particular therapy, and some exhibited the fine white line of a surgical scar with a commentary on how clean and tight the skin had grown back over the wound. But when patients finished with the details, they always moved to a more general, personal statement. For the experience of being healed penetrates deeper than the scalpel, and it permeates the self more thoroughly than any drug. There is a feeling of deliverance, a profound sense of renewal, a celebration that breaks into a chant: "I'm going home. I'm going home. I can hardly believe it, I'm going home."

These words and these feelings are a contemporary expression of the same force that drove the

woman to fall down before Jesus and tell him "the
whole truth" (Mark 5:33). Not just the truth about
her hemorrhage and not just the truth about her
secretive approach to him, but the whole truth.
The truth of her shame. The truth of her bitterness.
The truth of her desperation. And above all, the
truth of her faith. How she had hoped and believed
and how Jesus had fulfilled her hope and vin-
dicated her faith. Year after year she had prayed
like the psalmist—if not in word, then in spirit:

> Be gracious to me, O Lord, for I am languishing;
> O Lord, heal me, for my bones are troubled.
> My soul also is sorely troubled.
> But thou, O Lord—how long?
>
> (Ps. 6:2-3)

Now the Lord had answered her through Jesus.
Bones and soul were healed.

Bones and soul represent the entire person. The
troubled bones are the pain, the blood, the organic
dysfunction. The troubled soul is the distraught
self, the fear, the despair, the feeling that all life is
out of whack because the body is not functioning
the way it should. To heal the bones is to heal the
soul. This is "the whole truth" which the woman
had experienced in reaching out to Jesus and
which she now acknowledged to him on her knees.

The woman's response can also be ours. It was
the response of a surgeon who was himself operated on and who thanked God for working
through the skill of a colleague. It was the response
of an engineer who underwent a coronary bypass
and stopped by the church on the way home from
the hospital to join me in praising God that he had
made it through. Both were men of science. Precise
individuals with exacting skills. Neither man was
rejecting his technical training nor his sophis-

ticated understanding of the human body. Neither man saw a conflict between God's healing power and modern medicine. The second was an extension of the first. The accomplishments of the physicians and nurses were the evidence of God's presence. The surgeon and the engineer affirmed the same "whole truth" that the bleeding woman had encountered in Jesus who healed bones and soul alike.

THE OTHER SIDE OF PAIN

"And [Jesus] said to her, 'Daughter, your faith has made you well; go in peace, and be healed of your disease'" (Mark 5:34). Jesus addresses the woman as "Daughter." How that word must have sounded with rapture to her after so many years of being "the sick woman," "the bleeder," "the sinner"! She had reached out to Jesus to stop the bleeding, and now he had done more than that. He had taken her back into the human family.

Daughter. The intimacy of the word tells us that in our pain, through our pain, and beyond our pain is a healing and accepting power who addresses us with the same tenderness that a parent shows a child. When we first feel the lump in our bodies that never was there before or we hear the doctor speaking quietly to the nurse about tomorrow's tests, our minds are flooded with dreadful fantasies. Then we need to hear again this word: "Daughter." We need to sense that holy presence who never abandons us and who is speaking to us through every action that supports, restores, and accepts us.

"Your faith has made you well." Jesus, as did the woman earlier (v. 28), uses the word "saved" for

"made you well." The stopping of her hemorrhage
is an act of salvation. It has saved her from physical deterioration and psychological devastation.
However, something even greater than these victo-
ries is covered by the word "saved." The woman
has reached for Christ. Her extended arm is the
outward evidence of an interior motion. The physical reaching out that stopped her hemorrhage reflects the stretch of heart and mind that is required
to stop the bleeding of the human spirit.

The woman could have decided not to risk faith.
She could have given up. She had every reason to.
She had been afflicted with her damning condition
for twelve years. She had tried every treatment
available and spent her last cent in the pursuit of
health. Who could blame her for being bitter? Life
was a rotten deal. Why not find a few other people
in similar straits and spend the rest of their days
commiserating with one another?

But some gracious instinct told the woman that
such a course would only intensify the bleeding, if
not the physical bleeding, then at least the psychological bleeding. She and her cosufferers would
cover the same ground over and over: How the condition had started. How they had tried to stop it.
How the community rejected them. How unfair
life is. How unjust the ways of God are. If she went
through this litany of despair often enough, the
woman might bleed to death from self-pity before
her body succumbed to the loss of plasma and
hemoglobin.

Instead, she broke through the walls of her de-
spairing self through an action of faith. Salvation
is the divine prompting to extend ourselves beyond
ourselves in order to be healed. This extension is
not simply casting ourselves into the vastness of
existence. More is involved than affirming life. Sal-

vation is stretching the center of our self toward
the personal center of existence. We reach for
Christ.

The woman touched only Jesus' garments. She
made contact with the perimeter of his being
rather than with his body. But this was enough to
save her. Salvation does not require a total grasp-
ing of who Jesus is. Not even the most devoted disciple achieves that in a lifetime.

Salvation requires direction toward Christ, an
essential thrust toward his reality. If we only approach the outer limits of Christ's being, he will
reach the rest of the way to us. This is what he does
to the woman in his benediction: "Go in peace." He
gives to her more than she sought. She wanted the
blood to stop, and it did. But now he adds to it the
gift of peace. Like the stillness that steals upon us
after a fever has broken, a sense of well-being
moves into the woman's body. An awareness of restored life pulses in her heart. And a feeling of
renewed relationships between self, community,
and God shines like the welcome sun after a long,
damp night. She can go in peace. Peace with herself. Peace with others. Peace with the Lord.

"And be healed of your disease." These final
words may seem redundant since Jesus has already declared "Your faith has made you well." In
fact, they are not redundant at all. The primary
meaning of the word rendered "disease" is "whip"
or "scourge." The statement reveals a profound understanding of the experience of disease as torture
or punishment. This perception is echoed in the
patient's desperate questions: "Why is God doing
this to me?" "Why am I being tortured?" When we
are healed from a long chronic disease it is as
though someone removed us from the rack. Jesus
affirms this experience of utter relief. Perhaps the

literal translation of the King James Version captures best the spirit of the remark: "Be whole of thy
plague." To recover from the plague! This is the
ecstatic assurance that Jesus gives the woman. He
does not want her fretting about the future now
that she is liberated from the agony of the past. He
is telling her that she is "free for ever from this
trouble" (New English Bible).

Jesus' rhapsodic valediction sings the true pitch
of salvation. Salvation is the exhilaration of having
tubes and stitches removed. Salvation is walking
down the hall without growing faint and weak. Salvation is driving home from the hospital and noticing how well the tuberous begonias have done. Salvation is sitting in our favorite chair at home and
realizing—after our visitors have left and the family is (thankfully) a little less attentive—that in the
stillness someone is speaking to us. Perhaps not
words. Perhaps only a sense of intimacy and of
peace blended in unarticulated satisfaction.
Should we try to discern the message more precisely, it might well sound with this ancient echo:
"Daughter, your faith has made you well; go in
peace, and be healed of your disease."

Chapter 8

From Despair

The chief priests and the Pharisees still had the jitters. Their opponent was dead and buried, but they continued to be as anxious as when he was alive. Once more they made an appointment to see the governor: "Sir, we remember how that impostor said, while he was still alive, 'After three days I will rise again.' Therefore order the sepulchre to be made secure until the third day, lest his disciples go and steal him away, and tell the people, 'He has risen from the dead,' and the last fraud will be worse than the first" (Matt. 27:63-64).

The men's reasoning seemed plausible enough, but was it fear of a hoax that actually motivated their request? A deception can last only so long. Sooner or later someone spills the beans, and every effort at a cover-up increases the credibility gap between the perpetrators and the public. Perhaps what was eating away inside the priests and the Pharisees was the "fear that the man whom they had crucified would *really* come alive again as he had promised" (Frederick Buechner, *The Magnificent Defeat,* p. 76; Seabury Press, 1968). God might act in an unexpected way. God might raise the foolish carpenter from the dead. There might be a resurrection! Where would that leave the priestly establishment? What would happen to their pre-

eminent position in the community? To their familiar patterns of life and thought? To the sanc-
tified security of their religious scruples? What
would happen to their neat little systems if God did
something they could not explain? These were the
unspoken questions that made the religious leaders nervous and drove them to seek Pilate's help in
sealing the tomb and posting a guard of soldiers.
And they are the same unarticulated fears with
which we approach the resurrection.

Everything in life must make sense to us. By
"sense" we mean that it must fit into our world of
observation, prediction, and control. We will accept the resurrection if someone can explain with
the precision of a molecular biologist how the dead
cells were reanimated and the heart recharged
with energy and the lungs made to pump once
more. The resurrection is a threat to our closed
world view just as it was to that of the ancient
skeptics. The resurrection reveals the tenuous nature of every human system of thought.

Whenever established patterns of understanding are challenged, people rush to seal the tomb
and post a guard of soldiers. Religious people appeal to the Bible. Scientists question the reliability
of data that does not fit their theories. Politicians
fall back on clichés and old programs to address
new problems in society. All of us panic at the
thought that life might be turned into some new
and incomprehensible reality.

THE RADICAL EVENT IN PLAIN HUMAN DRESS

At the time of Christ's resurrection many people
were as skeptical as we are. And not only Jesus'
opponents! Many of his own disciples doubted be-

fore they believed. The first announcement of the resurrection "seemed to them an idle tale" (Luke 24:11). Thomas insisted, "Unless I see in his hands the print of the nails, and place my finger in the mark of the nails, and place my hand in his side, I will not believe" (John 20:25).

Easter was the radical event that made the gospel sound either foolish or intriguing or true. When Paul spoke in Athens about the risen Christ and the future resurrection of all people, "some mocked; ... others said, 'We will hear you again about this.' ... But some men joined him and believed" (Acts 17:32, 34).

Those who encountered Christ after Easter did not attempt to argue the incredulous into belief. Instead of explanations they offered experiences. They told what it was like to find Christ present and living among them. Their stories do not prove the resurrection, but they provide us with an intuitive feeling for how Christ was known. To reread these stories is to share again the early church's excitement and to identify how Christ continues to be present among us.

On the first Easter two disciples walked toward the village of Emmaus (Luke 24:13-35). They were bruised by the world's cruelty and injustice. Two days ago they had seen their best friend arrested, tried in a kangaroo court, tortured, and executed.

While the two men walked, a stranger joined them. They did not realize that it was their friend, and Jesus did nothing to make his identity known to them. He did not dazzle them with his risen presence. Instead, he listened to them. He entered their world. He probed what they were thinking and feeling: "What is this conversation which you are holding with each other as you walk?" (v. 17).

The two men unloaded the whole grisly tale on

the stranger. Only after they had poured out their
pain and bewilderment (vs. 19-24) did Jesus offer
his own perspective on what had happened: "And
beginning with Moses and all the prophets, he interpreted to them in all the scriptures the things
concerning himself" (v. 27).

When they got close to home, the disciples invited the stranger to join them for the night. They
sensed that he must "be going further" (v. 28)—
further than their house, further than their village,
further than the land and the sea beyond. Yet the
stranger was willing to join them. The greatness of
his destination did not make their own home too
humble a place for him to stop.

When they brought out supper, it seemed as
though the stranger were the host and they were
the guests. He offered grace, broke the bread and
passed it to them. It was just then—as he handed
the broken loaf across the table and they felt the
hardened crust in their hands—that "their eyes
were opened and they recognized him; and he vanished out of their sight" (v. 31).

Christ had appeared in the plainest human
dress: not as a celestial courier fluttering with
angel's wings in the ether of heaven, but as a stranger whose feet pounded the same clay road that the
two disciples walked. It was a miracle. It was a
radical event that uprooted their experience and
their understanding. The splintery wood, the punc-
tured body, and the sealed grave were no longer the
images that summarized the final truth of life.
Christ was with them. Christ was a stranger whom
they invited into their home and who passed the
bread at the table. Extraordinary power was present in an ordinary act. The transformation of a
dead carpenter into the risen Lord was confirmed

by their eyes which beheld him and by their hearts which burned within them (v. 32). Sitting down to supper with a stranger, they saw Christ.

Christ came to the two men of Emmaus in their common life, and that is how he continued to appear to the other disciples. Peter and many of his companions had returned to the workaday world of fishermen (John 21:1-14). Back to boats and nets, oars and sails, anchor lines and mainsheets. Yet when they returned to the job, things were not exactly as they had left them. There was still the hard labor of hauling in ropes and the frustration of an empty net after waiting hours for a catch. But there was also something else. A stranger appeared on shore and helped them with their work. From his vantage point on land he could see a school of fish that the water's glare blinded from their sight. Trusting his directions, they cast the net over the starboard side and made a tremendous catch. It was just then, as the weight of the lines burned the skin under their clamped knuckles, that the "disciple whom Jesus loved said to Peter, 'It is the Lord!' " (v. 7). Peter threw on his tunic, leaped overboard, and headed for Christ. The others, realizing that the net was too full to haul it over the gunwales, dragged it to shore with the boat. They could smell a campfire burning on the beach. Jesus was cooking a meal of fish and bread for them, and when they finished sorting their catch, he said, "Come and have breakfast" (v. 12).

Once again the radical event of Easter was known in plain human dress. Christ appeared in the same way as he had on the road to Emmaus: as a stranger who entered the disciples' world, who offered his own unique perspective, and who fed

them. Not in a moment of meditative ecstasy, but
while they were on the job, the disciples encountered their risen Lord.

DEATH AND RESURRECTION: HERE AND NOW

The plain and subdued character of Christ's resurrection appearances gave them a relevance to
daily life that more spectacular manifestations
would never have possessed. Because Christ was
known to the disciples in simple ways, they were
able to see how death and resurrection are experienced here and now. Christ's resurrection revealed to the early church patterns of human
transformation which take place in this life and
which are evidence of the same power that raised
Christ from the grave.

The church's resurrection understanding of life
pervaded its preaching and worship. When believers collected their memories of Jesus and his teaching, their experience of the risen Lord influenced
their language and deepened their understanding
of the parables. Luke works the language of death
and life into his telling of the parable of the prodi-
gal son (Luke 15:11-32). When the foolish boy returns home after blowing his wad in strange lands,
the father exclaims: "This my son was dead and is
alive again" (v. 24). The transformation from child
to adult, from rebellion to repentance, is a resurrection. Every time we refashion our lives to accept
the love that brought us into being there is a resurrection. Resurrection is returning home to God. It
is affirming our personal connection and obliga-
tion to be source of all that is.

The first requirement of resurrection is death.
We cannot choose life without choosing the death

of our old selves. We prefer to ooze our way into new life, to make tiny adjustments that do not threaten who we are or how we live. The foolish boy of the parable does not instantly return to his father when his fortunes fail. First he tries to make it on his own: "He went and joined himself to one of the citizens of that country, who sent him into his fields to feed swine. And he would gladly have fed on the pods that the swine ate; and no one gave him anything" (vs. 15-16). Before the young man can face the embarrassment of returning home he has to experience the desperation of his situation. Only then is he ready to acknowledge that he needs his father: "But when he came to himself he said, 'How many of my father's hired servants have bread enough and to spare, but I perish here with hunger! I will arise and go to my father, and I will say to him, "Father, I have sinned against heaven and before you; I am no longer worthy to be called your son; treat me as one of your hired servants"'" (vs. 17-19).

The young man's words represent a death as real as our heart's last beat and our lungs' last breath. It is the death of our pride, the death of our belief that we can make it through life entirely on our own.

Like all death, it is scary. We do not want to release control over our lives. We wonder what lies beyond the decision to give up our old way of life. The parable answers this fear: "And [the young man] arose and came to his father. But while he was yet at a distance, his father saw him and had compassion, and ran and embraced him and kissed him" (v. 20). On the other side of death is a welcoming love. God runs to greet us before we reach God. We feel the divine approach in the peace that comes when we decide to admit our guilt. We sense

the divine presence in the breeze that blows
through our psychic rooms which had been choked
with the stale air of our pride. We reclaim our relationship to the truth that created us. We bury our
old ways of thinking and acting and find stirring in
our lives a power for new thought and new action.
It is God speaking to us through the internal motions of our own spirits: "This my son was dead and
is alive again" (v. 24).

Paul the apostle describes the resurrection more
as a future event than as a current reality. "For if
we have been united with [Christ] in a death like
his, we *shall* certainly be united with him in a
resurrection like his" (Rom. 6:5, emphasis added).
Nevertheless, Paul also experienced the power of
the resurrection here and now. It came across to
him as the resilience of life. The resurrection was
a coiled steel spring of hope wound up in his heart
that uncurled with irrepressible power driving
Paul beyond defeat and disillusionment: "We are
afflicted in every way, but not crushed; perplexed,
but not driven to despair; persecuted, but not forsaken; struck down, but not destroyed; always car-
rying in the body the death of Jesus, so that the life
of Jesus may also be manifested in our bodies" (II
Cor. 4:8-10).

Resurrection is being "afflicted in every way, but
not crushed." I recall a woman who suffered from
arthritis. Pained and crippled, she always responded to questions about herself as briefly as possible. "Not very well, but I'll make it, thank you.
And what about yourself? What are you doing?
What's going on now? Have some tea and cookies.
I could hardly wait for you to come, because I want
to hear all about you." That's resurrection here and
now.

Resurrection is being "perplexed, but not driven

to despair." I once knew a social worker who ran a settlement house and was involved in the local political scene. When city officials sabotaged her efforts to help unemployed youth, she was baffled by their behavior. But she did not despair. Through shrewd organization and an appeal to the community, she maintained and expanded her program. That's resurrection here and now.

Resurrection is being "persecuted, but not forsaken." I think of a black professor from South Africa who is under constant threat from that oppressive regime. When asked why he did not cave in under the pressure, he said: "I feel the presence of my people who are joined with me in this struggle. We trust God is with us." That's resurrection here and now.

Resurrection is being "struck down, but not destroyed." I can picture a farmer, one of whose arms was mangled in a thresher, who used to cut the hay in the field next to my house. After he lost his arm, he still threw the bales up on the wagon. He picked up each bale with his single arm and swung it back and forth until it gained enough momentum to be raised shoulder high. Then he bent his knees and quickly got underneath the bale with his whole body. Finally, he thrust himself like a shot-putter toward the wagon and heaved the seventy-five pounds of compressed hay into place. Then on to the next bale. Swing. Dip. Thrust. And the next bale. Swing. Dip. Thrust. And the next bale. Swing. Dip. Thrust. That's resurrection here and now.

All these people—the arthritic woman, the social worker, the black professor, the one-armed farmer —carried in their bodies the death of Jesus. Each was scarred by the same destructive force that had killed Jesus and pursued Paul throughout his ministry. Yet that power was not ultimately decisive.

Greater than the pain of swollen joints, greater than
the betrayal of politicians, greater than the oppression of tyrants, greater than the terror of skin and
muscle lost to whirling metal was a force for hope,
for compassion, for justice, and for strength. It was
"the life of Jesus ... manifested in [their] bodies." It
was the same power that ruptured the grave at
Easter and now cracked the rock of pain and injustice. It was resurrection here and now.

Life is a series of deaths and resurrections: Disease and healing. Estrangement and reconciliation. Despair and hope. Loss and recovery. Both
death and resurrection are familiar characters in
our everyday existence. Death is that faceless
figure with whom we wrestle all our lives, in our
fear and in our darkness. And resurrection is the
grasp of heaven's hand that releases death's chok-
ing grip. Resurrection is our daily sense of renewal.
Resurrection is our passion for justice. Resurrection is the force that will enable us to get out of bed
and face tomorrow's struggles even if today has
been devastating.

MORE THAN METAPHOR

Resurrection is part of our common life. But that
does not mean it is merely a metaphor for the tri-
umph of the human spirit. If resurrection is only a
simile for the resurgent strength of the psyche, and
if death is the final reality of existence, then life is
a mockery. The tea poured with an arthritic hand
and the bale of hay picked up with a single arm
tease us with the semblance of victory when our
defeat is already decided. Unless death itself is
finally vanquished, every battle that we win over
the terrors of existence will be erased by the grave.

"If Christ has not been raised, then our preaching is in vain and your faith is in vain. . . . If for this life only we have hoped in Christ, we are of all men most to be pitied" (I Cor. 15:14, 19).

Paul viewed the resurrection as the indispensable underpinning of the entire gospel. Without the resurrection, all other forms of salvation—liberation, security, creating, exorcism, forgiveness, healing—would appear as flickers of light destined to sputter out in the darkness of an eternal night.

Our society is in terror of such a night. This fear is written in the face of popular culture and its frantic pursuit for a salvation of bliss. A recent book, typical of the genre discussed on talk shows and found next to the cashier's rack in supermarkets, promises: "You *can* live happily ever after!" Paul's description of his daily existence—"afflicted in every way, but not crushed"—is more realistic than the adolescent fantasy of perpetual pleasure. Paul is closer to the nerve of life than the wisdom of contemporary society because he does not deny death. Resurrection, unlike "living happily ever after," embraces death as a necessary element in the transformation of existence.

Resurrection even recognizes the sadness of death. "Jesus wept" (John 11:35) before the raising of Lazarus. He did not say: "Cheer up, everyone. Death is not real." For those who believe in resurrection, death is still scary and sad. If it were not, then it would cease to be death, and resurrection as the transformation of death into life would make no sense.

"Living happily ever after" is the illusion that drives us from one self-improvement program to another. New Year's resolutions, health kicks, and plunges into self-renewal are short-lived. The psyche grows tired. We cannot resurrect ourselves. Attempts at remaking our lives that are confined to the boundaries of human potential fizzle out because they demand more from the self than it can deliver. We need a force more powerful, more persistent, and more pervasive than our sporadic commitments to changing ourselves and how we live. The resurrected Christ is that power.

Paul the apostle reminds the Corinthians that through the good news of Christ's death and resurrection "You are saved" (I Cor. 15:2). A more accurate translation is: "You are being saved." Salvation is the continuing transformation of human life that is initiated and sustained by Christ's rising from the dead. Every time that human life is lifted up to a higher, healthier, more hopeful state of being, Christ is present. Sometimes he may be explicitly acknowledged and other times ignored. But if there has been a genuine transformation, a death and a resurrection, then Christ is there in power if not in name.

Because resurrection is part of our daily lives, we trust that it shall also be a reality on the other side of the grave. The moist fingers of the Spirit which first molded the clay vessels of our bodies are every day reshaping our hearts and minds. God's skilled hands know every contour of our being. They keep smoothing the rough surfaces of our hatred and repairing the cracks caused by tragedy and despair. And when we die, those same confident hands shall turn again the potter's wheel and refashion who we are into what we ought to be.

VICTORY

Christ's resurrection turns life into a victory. Victory, not success. The two are not the same. Success means bringing to a prosperous conclusion our own endeavors. Success is the crowning accomplishment in our culture. There is no greater accolade than to be deemed successful and no more damning an indictment than to be adjudged a failure.

Victory is different. Victory means final superiority in any struggle or battle. Common speech preserves the distinction between the terms. The losing team in a game may make many successful plays, but only the winning team is victorious. If a patient dies, the medical treatment is called a failure although the family may refer to the person's victory over pain and despair.

Jesus was a failure. His execution as a criminal was for many people the decisive argument against accepting him as the Messiah. That someone who was hanged on a cross should claim their loyalty struck thoughtful folk as absurd. The very idea of it was "a stumbling block to Jews and folly to Gentiles" (I Cor. 1:23).

We, like those first-century skeptics, also want our religion to be respectable and reasonable. We too "demand signs" (I Cor. 1:22). Before we look up to people we want to know: What do they do in life? What's their position? Whom do they know? If someone suggested that the person most worthy of our adoration and allegiance was a working-class man who had been executed in an electric chair, we would consider it the prattle of a fool. We would come close to feeling the same way as the original, ancient doubters of the gospel.

We also "seek wisdom" (I Cor. 1:22). We want a sane, balanced understanding of reality—not one that is soiled with the blood of execution and that ruffles our peace with a nasty scene of violence.

If Christ had possessed the signs that we demand

and the wisdom that we seek, then he would have been a success. He would fit neatly into our scheme of values. Today we might recall how there once lived an outstanding religious teacher named Jesus. He had a fine way with a story and related well to everyone. His pleasant manner and his deep human wisdom carved a warm spot in the hearts of many. If ever you are in Jerusalem, you might want to stop by his grave and honor a great man of old.

"But in fact Christ has been raised from the dead, the first fruits of those who have fallen asleep" (I Cor. 15:20). Death is not defeat. In Christ we already have the first evidence that when all hope is lost and our lives are finished, just then we have more reason to hope than ever.

Christ's victory works through our sorrow. I recall a family whose teen-age son died in an accident about a month before Easter. They made a daily trek to his grave during the first few weeks of their grief. Usually they placed some flowers there. It so happened that the cemetery had been chosen for an ecumenical sunrise service which I was to lead that Easter. When the great day came, our early spring disapperared and there was an inch of snow and a raw, wet wind. A hearty congregation stood in ski parkas on top of the cemetery's highest hill and sang "Jesus Christ Is Risen Today." About fifty yards away was the boy's new grave. The flowers had been blown to pieces and dead, brown petals were scattered over the snow. Among the bundled faithful stood the grieving family, sorrow still in their faces but singing the glad words of the hymn. The glory of the blossoms had vanished, and only the seasonless power of Christ's resurrection made possible their song.

The family was "struck down, but not de-

stroyed." Mixed together with their tears and their
emptiness was a hope that not even six feet of cold
clay could suffocate. Resurrection did not save
them from mourning; it saved them from mourning as people "who have no hope" (I Thess. 4:13).
Salvation is the victory of the resurrection. Salvation is pouring out our hearts in grief while singing the Easter hymn. Salvation is watching brown
petals blow across a spring snowfall and knowing
that there is a power for new life that never fades
and never dies. Salvation is weeping yet trusting
that someday "God himself will be with [us]; he will
wipe away every tear from [our] eyes, and death
shall be no more, neither shall there be mourning
nor crying nor pain any more" (Rev. 21:3-4).

THE TRUMPET SHALL SOUND

The hope of resurrection sustains more than the
family whose shoes are caked with the mud of the
grave. God's resurrection power is the energy
source that can revitalize a culture when its symbols of meaning have died. Nearly two thousand
years ago the risen Christ whirled the dynamo of
faith and prevented a blackout of hope during the
nightfall of the Roman Empire.

Today our civilization needs to be recharged by
that same power which made the ancient world
leap with new life. We do not need a resuscitation
of the past, we need a resurrection of the present:
a transformation of ourselves, our values, our institutions, our symbols of meaning. There is a universal longing for this metamorphosis, but no one is
able to bring it about. We fumble with the control
dials on our machines. We tinker with meditation
and psychology. We grope for leaders who can lead

us to the light. But we act from desperation rather than faith. We need to believe again in the resurrection: to trust that the structures of existence can be rearranged and re-formed into a new and vital reality. Ezekiel had the resurrection vision. Looking over a devastated Israel, he saw a valley of dry bones (Ezek., ch. 37). That's what we are—dry bones. Our dreams of justice, our ideals of freedom, our institutions of education and government, have calcified and grown brittle. Our talk about the "impersonalization," the "dehumanization," and the "bureaucratization" of modern life is our modern lingo for dry bones.

"Can these bones live?" (Ezek. 37:3).

Yes. They can live. Not because of our power, but because there is a dynamic force transmitted from the center and source of being that can revitalize the dead elements of existence. "Thus says the Lord God to these bones: Behold I cause breath to enter you, and you shall live. And I will lay sinews upon you, and will cause flesh to come upon you, and cover you with skin, and put breath in you, and you shall live; and you shall know that I am the Lord" (Ezek. 37:5-6).

To hear God speaking to our bones and to believe in the possibilities of resurrection is to be raised up ourselves. It is to be "born anew to a living hope through the resurrection of Jesus Christ from the dead" (I Peter 1:3). A living hope! A hope that races through the arteries of our intellect and our imagination. A hope that impels us to undertake new experiments, to develop new theories, to create new works of art, to search for new ways of feeding the hungry and empowering the poor. We give ourselves with abandon to working on what once seemed insurmountable. For we believe in the resurrection. Since death itself is to be "swallowed up in victory" (I Cor. 15:54), we struggle against the rest of life's dark forces confident of victory. Even if our particular efforts for justice, for health, and for peace fail, we do not despair. We know that someday "we shall all be changed, in a moment, in the twinkling of an eye, at the last trumpet. For the trumpet will sound, and the dead will be raised imperishable, and we shall be changed" (I Cor. 15: 51-52).

The trumpet of justice shall sound. And the victims of war and dungeon and concentration camp shall be restored to their loved ones. All torment shall cease, and tyrants shall rule no more.

The trumpet of life shall sound. And those whose bodies were racked with disease and suffering shall know a perfect wholeness.

The trumpet of love shall sound. And all who were despised and rejected and lonely shall be embraced by the arms of everlasting compassion.

The trumpet of celebration shall sound. And all who starved shall be fed at the banquet table of the King and nourished with eternal strength.

This is the vision of victory that moves us to stand our ground against every evil and injustice. All that we presently hear of heaven's future trumpet is a distant note of glory. Now and then it penetrates to our hearts—at the birth of a child or the discovery of a galaxy or the finale of a symphony. These intermittent echoes assure us that someday the celestial trumpet shall burst into thunderous sound and we shall arise and go home to God forever.

Chapter 9

From Blindness

I never was fond of the painting. It was an anemic watercolor of trees in pastel golds and grays. I knew the late-fall feeling that the artist was after, but still the colors were so pale that the picture did not hold together. It seemed as vapid as the last evening light that hangs in a November sky and is blotted from the horizon by the landscape and the night. The painting looked like a smudge hanging on the wall in our dining room.

Then my friend Oscar reframed the picture. He put an earthen-brown matting around it which brought out a similar shade that was lurking in the background but that I had never before noticed. This brown, subtly intersected by lattices of twig and leaf, reached from one side of the painting to the other. It gave the picture coherence and the trees strength. I found myself going in the dining room and looking at the picture to enjoy its color and life. It had turned from a smudge into one of my favorite paintings.

Worship, like Oscar's matting, is a way of framing life to make us aware of God's presence. Worship draws our eyes to the acts of salvation that are part of life but that are easily missed. By making God the dominant color of our existence, formal acts of praise reveal how God is the subtler shade of being which gives everyday life its coherence and vitality. When we hear that "in the name of Jesus Christ we are forgiven," then we reflect on how our neighbor forgave us and realize that God was there. When the Scripture lesson tells how God healed people in the ancient past, then we remember our recovery from an operation and realize that God was there. When we sing "Holy, Holy, Holy," then we recall the sight of fresh snow balanced on the million needles of a fir tree and realize that God was there. Worship sharpens our perception. It turns life from a smudge of disordered experience into a picture that has clarity and strength. Worship is salvation because it makes us conscious of how God is saving us in our everyday life and thereby lets us appropriate and affirm that saving power.

FIRST MEMORIES

The psalmists frame the history of Israel with praise and thanksgiving. Their pictures of God's salvation are not like the somber portraits of corporation presidents that hang in boardrooms. But rather they are spirited visions from the past that make a living claim on the present:

O give thanks to the Lord, for he is good,
for his steadfast love endures for ever:
. . . .
to him who smote the first-born of Egypt,
for his steadfast love endures for ever;
and brought Israel out from among them,
for his steadfast love endures for ever;
with a strong hand and an outstretched arm,
for his steadfast love endures for ever;
to him who divided the Red Sea in sunder,

for his steadfast love endures for ever;
and made Israel pass through the midst of it,
   for his steadfast love endures for ever;
but overthrew Pharaoh and his host in the Red Sea,
   for his steadfast love endures for ever;
to him who led his people through the wilderness,
   for his steadfast love endures for ever.

(Ps. 136:1, 10-16)

This particular psalm may have been spoken an-
tiphonally. The priest read the first half of each
verse, and the congregation offered the refrain.
Every scene from Israel's history heightens the
awareness of God's continuing presence: "For his
steadfast love endures for ever." God not only
"overthrew Pharaoh" once upon a time, God continues to liberate Israel now. Through worship the
past lives in the present. What God did becomes
what God does. And this pattern holds true in the
psalms for nearly every form of salvation that we
have discussed.

Security, creation, forgiveness, and healing are
not the ancient acts of a God whose joints have
grown stiff with age and who no longer has the
exuberance to fashion a universe or establish a nation. The worshipers in the Jerusalem Temple recall those first memories of salvation in order to
celebrate that God is working as energetically
today as yesterday:

O give thanks to the God of gods,
   for his steadfast love endures for ever:
. . . .
to him who alone *does* great wonders,
   for his steadfast love endures for ever;
to him who by understanding made the heavens,
   for his steadfast love endures for ever;
to him who spread out the earth upon the waters,
   for his steadfast love endures for ever;

> to him who made the great lights,
>   for his steadfast love endures for ever;
> the sun to rule over the day,
>   for his steadfast love endures for ever;
> the moon and stars to rule over the night,
>   for his steadfast love endures for ever.
>   (Ps. 136:2, 4-9, emphasis added)

The same God who macramed the DNA double helix molecule and threw quasars into space is busy braiding new chains of molecules and compacting black holes between the palms of his hands. "For his steadfast love endures for ever."

The first memories of a worshiping community function the same way as our childhood memories: they form our identity and our patterns of adult behavior. Betty Ford recalls her first memory in these words: "I was either two or three in my mother's arms on the front porch of our summer cottage by a lake in Michigan. A summer storm was approaching, and mother—I can still see her doing this—pressed me closer to her while saying, over and over again, how nice it was going to be, how beautiful the storm was going to be. To this day I like an approaching storm and dark water and the thunder and the lightning. My mother was, of course, terrified of storms, but she didn't want me to be, and I'm not" (*The New York Times Magazine,* Oct. 26, 1975). Ancient Israel's first memory was similar. The nation had been held in God's everlasting arms through the storms of the exodus and the settlement of the Promised Land. This primary experience of care and protection forever after shaped who Israel was. Through worship the Israelites celebrated how God had nursed them from a scraggly band of runaway slaves into a nation.

Worship was salvation because it reminded the

Israelites of their identity. Who were they? They
were a group of people whom God loved. No matter
what the surrounding culture said about them, no
matter what happened in world politics, no matter
how institutions and values shifted, the Israelites
reaffirmed their identity through worship: a people
loved by God.

Worship was also salvation because it reminded
the Israelites what God expected of them. How
were they to live? They were to do justice, to live
holy lives, to be a light in a dark world. Amid the
confusion of fertility cults and idolatry they re-
called in worship that "the law of the Lord is perfect, reviving the soul; the testimony of the Lord is
sure, making wise the simple" (Ps. 19:7). In worship the Israelites regained the moral focus of their
lives: obedience to God's law.

The memories of Israel's worship were no nos-
talgia trip. They were not an attempt to escape to
the good old days when God hit the dusty trail and
there was the high adventure of striking out for the
Promised Land. Rather, the memories were a way
of claiming strength for the present and the future.
The memories were passed on through the community of faith so that each succeeding generation
might still feel the protection of the everlasting
arms:

> We will not hide them from their children,
>   but tell to the coming generation
> the glorious deeds of the Lord, and his might,
>   and the wonders which he has wrought.
> He established a testimony in Jacob,
>   and appointed a law in Israel,
> which he commanded our fathers
>   to teach to their children;
> that the next generation might know them,
>   the children yet unborn,

and arise and tell them to their children,
  so that they should set their hope in God,
and not forget the works of God,
  but keep his commandments.

                                              (Ps. 78:4-7)

In our individualistic society corporate worship
has become problematic in a way it never was for
the ancient Israelites. Because each person is intensely concerned about his or her own identity,
the saving power of community memory has weakened. We are reduced to individual life stories.
What was my childhood like? What was yours like?
We tell each other our private first memories, but
we do not celebrate together our group memory.
The analyst's couch replaces the altar. Although
the exploration of private memory is often therapeutic, it cannot save a community. It cannot provide a corporate identity and a commitment to a
common moral law.

Without disposing of the couch, we need to reclaim the altar. We need to remember how God has
loved and continues to love not just "me" but all of
us. This corporate affirmation is ultimately helpful
to the individual, for it multiplies the streams that
feed the memory. We draw from the mighty river
of the entire community as well as from the shal-
lower creeks of our private existence. When our
personal memories run dry of love and care, we
can still be filled by the community.

I recall a man whose marriage was unsteady,
whose business partner had deserted him, and
whose small child was in the hospital. He came to
church drained of all his personal resources. Even
the man's faith in God was to no avail, because he
could not believe that God had let his private world
collapse. But when he heard the words of Scripture, sang the hymns, joined in the responsive

readings and the unison prayers, he found new
strength. Worship reminded him that reality was
larger than his private world. The community's
memory and celebration assured him of God's love
when he saw no evidence of it within the limits of
his own vision. On that Sunday, for that man, worship was salvation.

THE REMEMBRANCE OF A FINAL MEAL

In ancient Israel the most precious memory was
the exodus. In the early church it was Christ's Last
Supper and the promise of his coming again. Paul
records the church's first worship tradition: "The
Lord Jesus on the night when he was betrayed took
bread, and when he had given thanks, he broke it
and said . . ." (I Cor. 11:23-24). Astonishing words
these are—especially the contrast between "betrayed" and "thanks." We do not give thanks when
we are betrayed. We curse! Let a neighbor utter an
indiscreet word behind our backs, let a colleague
slant a report to the boss so it reflects unfavorably
on us, let a friend cool the relationship between us,
let us feel deserted by someone we depended on,
and see if we give thanks.

But on the night when Jesus was betrayed, on the
night when one of his associates would make a
bundle by turning him over to his enemies, on the
night when his closest followers would hightail it
for safety, on the night when the police would beat
him up, on the night when Jesus' dearest friend
would deny ever knowing him, on *that* night Jesus
gave thanks. That's worship. That's salvation.
Pouring out gratitude simply because you exist.
Being glad for a last meal with people who mean
a great deal to you. Rejoicing for the bread on the

table and the wine in the cup. Giving thanks even
though you are betrayed.

The astonishing words continue: "This is my
body which is broken for you" (I Cor. 11:24, margin). Body. It means more than the corpuscular
mass of cells whose elbows are resting on the table.
It means the entire being, the whole person. It
means Jesus with his voice raspy from preaching
to large crowds and his hands nicked and calloused
from working in a carpenter's shop since boyhood.
This broken bread represents all of Jesus: his life,
his teaching, his healing, his personality, his ministry. The bread is an expression of his heart,
opened so we can be sustained by its love. His mind,
revealed so we can be enlightened by its wisdom.
His soul, disclosed so we can discover our humanity through his humanity. His body, shattered so we
can be moved to justice and to take a stand for what
is right.

"This cup is the new covenant in my blood. Do
this, as often as you drink it, in remembrance of
me" (I Cor. 11:25). The blood is life. Vitality. Energy. Power. Zeal. It is the passion for a world made
right with God and with itself no matter what personal sacrifice is involved. It is the anger that
drives us to demolish injustice. It is the love that
impels us to reach out to the starving, the lonely,
the brutalized, the oppressed.

Christ's life surging through us fortifies our
identity and clarifies how we are to live. Who are
we? We are people whom Christ loved so intensely
that he was willing to die for us. How are we to live?
Even as Christ did: breaking open ourselves to others and pouring out our lives in service.

We lift a cup of wine to our lips and taste love in
our hearts. It is the awareness of a new relationship between ourselves and God—"the new cove-

nant." The covenant is not a legal document filled
out in triplicate, hemmed in with conditional
clauses, and filed at a county clerk's office in
heaven. A written agreement could no more ex-
press the spirit of our new relationship with God
than a marriage license can capture the essence of
a happy marriage. Only something as intimate yet
social as a meal together can suggest the character
of the covenant that Christ has established. The
covenant is a friendship, not a contract.

We may consider a legal agreement more bind-
ing than the unwritten understanding between
friends. But if we examine our deepest friendships,
we discover a commitment more permanently
etched on our hearts than any contract written on
vellum and signed with indelible ink (cf. II Cor.
3:3). Friendship is a matter of spirit rather than
law. And that's the kind of relationship, or "new
covenant," we have with Christ.

Christ calls us his friends (John 15:14,15), and he
invites us to have supper with him. We relish the
company as well as the meal. We share our sorrow,
and our host understands. We tell glad stories, and
our host rejoices. We confide our fears, and our host
puts us at ease. We leave the table satisfied because
we have fed on more than bread and wine. We have
feasted on what every human being thirsts and
hungers for: understanding, compassion, reassurance.

FLIMSY BREAD AND WATERY WINE

Many people today consider the Lord's Supper
more an antiquated ritual than a hearty meal, for
the consumer society has modified our understanding of eating and thereby altered our perception of

Communion. Our model meals are no longer a family gathered around a table. We drive up to plastic food factories, push a remote-control speaker, and order a double burger and fries. Food is a commodity. It comes like a hair dryer or an electric drill that we buy at a department store—encased in a box and submerged in a bag. Lacking the Creator's distinctive wrapping of blossoms, seeds, and leaves, food no longer appears to be a gift from God. Eating is consumption, not Communion. Our fast-food life-style weakens the underlying cultural reinforcement of a shared meal that originally lay behind the institution of the Last Supper.

Unfortunately, the worship of many Protestant churches has abetted the breakdown in our understanding of Communion. By holding the Lord's Supper infrequently and by stressing its private rather than communal character, the church's first memory has become hazy.

The atrophy of the family meal and the church's neglect of the Lord's Table have dimmed the ebullient, festive spirit that first characterized Christian worship: "And day by day, attending the temple together and breaking bread in their homes, they partook of food with glad and generous hearts, praising God and having favor with all the people" (Acts 2:46-47).

We have turned the firmly grained loaf and the heady brew of Christ's Meal into the flimsy bread and watery wine of privatized worship. As the ruling lay officer of a local church once told me: "I never look to the pews around me but keep my eyes straight ahead so as not to be distracted during Communion." As though Christ's sisters and brothers were a distraction! The joy of the Lord's Supper, as of any meal, is in sharing it. I recall traveling alone in Holland. I had finished supper by myself, and as I got up to leave the restaurant, a young man invited me to have coffee and dessert with him. I sat down and as we broke into an easy conversation, I found myself relishing the cake that he ordered more than anything else I had eaten that evening.

We need to reclaim the meal-like quality of Christian worship. Even if we do not celebrate Communion at every service, the rhythm and the melody of our worship can sing with the themes of the Last Supper:

Thanksgiving.
Feeding.
Remembering.
Proclaiming.

No matter what happens to us—disappointment, affliction, betrayal—we can give thanks. We can affirm the glories of daily existence: Hearing a favorite song on the radio. Passing someone on the street who waves to us. Receiving a personal letter when all we expected were bills. Noticing how our knees shape the bedcovers into a saddle-backed mountain like the one we climbed long ago with our family. As surely as Christ gave thanks on the night of his betrayal, we can respond with gratitude to the fact that we exist. Breath and pulse and the power to wiggle our toes and close our hands are gifts worthy of exultant thanks. To live is to receive from God. And to worship God is simply to respond with wonder and appreciation to the source of our being.

After giving thanks, we break open God's word and feed upon it. If that word is not present to us through the elements of bread and wine, we still receive it through Scripture, sermon, and prayer.

We listen to the word in the readings from the Bible. We acknowledge its personal claim on us in sermon and liturgy. We reach for its power through prayer. Worship is always a meal. It is a time when we feed on the riches of the Spirit and delight in the company of others who have gathered to take part in the same feast of love and faith.

All Christian worship is done "in remembrance" of Christ. Every prayer is offered in his name. Every action and hymn calls to mind his life of service and sacrifice. Like the ancient celebrations in the Jerusalem Temple, the remembrance of Christian worship is more than fingering through an old postcard album whose scenes from yesteryear bring a warm glow to the heart. The gospel pictures of Christ have not yellowed with age so as to soften their bold lines or mute their sharp message. We remember Christ's life, death, and resurrection because they make our own lives crackle with meaning. His struggles for the poor give us courage to persist in our own efforts for justice. His suffering helps us to endure our own pain. His death illuminates the mine shafts of our sin and the depths of God's love. His resurrection and return rescue the present and the future from the blight of hopelessness.

"For as often as you eat this bread and drink the cup, you proclaim the Lord's death until he comes" (I Cor. 11:26). As often as we give thanks, as often as we feed on God's word, as often as we remember Jesus Christ, we proclaim to the world the love of God. Worship is proclamation, and proclamation is consciousness-raising. Just as different groups hold conventions and lead seminars in order to firm up their identity and to make the larger society conscious of their opinions, so Christian worship arouses the world to an awareness of Jesus

Christ. Worship heightens our consciousness of our sin and of God's grace. It makes us confident of our identity as God's children. And it propels us into action on behalf of God's Kingdom. Worship is a statement of more than who we are and what we stand for. It is a proclamation of who God is and what God requires: "To do justice, and to love kindness, and to walk humbly with [our] God" (Micah 6:8).

IN A GOTHIC CATHEDRAL AND AT THE KITCHEN TABLE

Thanksgiving.
Feeding.
Remembering.
Proclaiming.

Through these acts of worship we feel the pulse of existence beating in our lives. The Spirit may lead people to arrange these elements of praise and nurture into different liturgical patterns, but underneath the form throbs the same divine heart. God has not mimeographed a single service of worship that is to be used at all times and in all places. God seeks everyone who is prepared to worship "in spirit and truth" (John 4:23,24).

Let people chant their adoration "in spirit and truth" beneath the vaulted arches of a Gothic cathedral, and God shall accept their worship.

Let people meet "in spirit and truth" in a white steepled church to sing their hymns and rededicate their lives, and God shall receive their offering.

Let people gather outdoors "in spirit and truth" to reflect on the wonders of God's creation, and God shall rejoice at their praise.

Let people keep silence "in spirit and truth" or let them clap their hands and stomp their feet "in spirit and truth," and God shall be glad for both the silence and the noise. Let people "in spirit and truth" say grace at the kitchen table, and God shall be pleased with their simplest words. Let all of life be framed by worship that is "in spirit and truth," and we shall become ourselves an offering pleasing in the Lord's sight.

Worship is salvation, because worship puts us in touch with reality as it actually is. Sometimes we think of it just the other way around: worship creates a pretty little retreat in the midst of a violent, ugly world. Worship is an antique that has been passed on through the ages and that we keep stored in the corner of our lives. We treasure its associations, but we don't consider its value for our common life. Evidently the Samaritan woman at the well thought along these lines. She knew about formal worship, its history and tradition. She told Jesus, "Our fathers worshiped on this mountain; and you say that in Jerusalem is the place where men ought to worship" (John 4:20).

What the woman did not know was how genuine worship extends beyond the sanctuary, beyond the holy mountain, into the fiber and substance of our daily existence. Her own life was a disaster—five different husbands and she was now living with a man she wasn't married to. Her worship life needed more than historical continuity with the past; it needed a personal connection to the present. That is why Jesus told the woman, "True worshipers will worship the Father in spirit and truth" (John 4:23). He wanted her to see that worship is not decided by its form or location—Jerusalem or Samaria, Gothic cathedral or kitchen table.

True worship is like the well in the field where Jesus met the restless woman. It creates within us "a spring of water welling up to eternal life" (John 4:14). This redeeming truth bubbles through the caked crust of our lives. It transforms the wasteland of our private existence and of society with its ancient feuds between Samaritans and Judeans, blacks and whites, rich and poor.

Regular worship keeps the spring cleaned out and flowing free. We return again and again to have the clear, cold water of truth splash us awake from the somnolent illusions of this world.

Worship is salvation because it braces us to deal with the reality of our entire lives. We no longer frame our existence with desperation and deception but with spirit and truth. We take a long, deep drink from the well of God's being and walk boldly into the future.

Chapter 10

God Says Yes

Salvation is Jesus Christ. An absurd statement. How can a person be salvation? We have seen that salvation is an event or an experience. A group of slaves escape to freedom. A tormented individual finds peace. Someone is forgiven. Salvation happens. Yet we do not usually describe people as happenings. If someone strikes our fancy in a restaurant, we do not say, "Look at that happening sitting two tables over." We say: "Look at that man in the brown-check sport coat. Isn't he an interesting-looking person?"

But if we probe beneath the immediate contrast between happenings and people, we discover that the most central events of our lives were particular individuals. The experiences that liberated and healed us—that "saved" us—were people who loved us in distinctive and highly personal ways: grandparents who visited their grandchildren every Sunday and brought smoked eel and Dutch almond cookies; an aunt who only saw her nephew during the summer but who in February sent him a five-dollar bill wrapped in a letter written on blue stationery; a music teacher who relished playing unaccompanied flute duets with his fumble-fingered student.

We cannot separate the special people in our

lives from our particular associations with them, from the unique way they touched us. They represent to us the embodiment of ideas and values that would otherwise be blown about in the turbulence of our minds, like milkweed dancing frenziedly in the wind. Jesus Christ is salvation because he affects us in the same way as the special people in our lives. He embodies the dynamics of salvation so that they do not become vague thoughts carried away by whatever doubt or fad is breezing through our lives.

But how can an ancient carpenter from an obscure village save us today? How can Jesus Christ still liberate us? Make us secure? Turn us into new creations? Drive out our demons? Forgive us? Heal us? Resurrect our lives? Inspire our worship? Christ saves us today the same way he saved people during his earthly ministry:

Through his personality.
Through his power.
Through his purpose.
Through his presence.

These are not theological abstractions. They are aspects of Christ's being that continue to penetrate our lives. They are expressions of a living Lord who is still saving this world.

SALVATION THROUGH CHRIST'S PERSONALITY

We usually use the word "personality" to mean an individual's temperament. However, when we speak of Christ's personality, the word refers to something more profound than his disposition. The word points to the character of Christ as it impinges on the depths of human nature. Christ's character is the central element in the structure of existence. It is not a feeling or a molecule in the brain, but it is the quintessential arrangement of life that makes us respond with greater intensity to another human being than to abstract truth. We are more excited when someone says "I love you" than when we read "Love is a great virtue," because the ultimate structure of reality is a personality rather than a principle. And that personality is Christ.

When we say that Jesus Christ is salvation we mean that we discover our true being through identification with the essential character of existence. We are led to this realization not by our own struggles but by Christ's personality encountering us in the center of our lives.

Christ reveals himself to us in many different ways. Sometimes he enters our life like light flashing from heaven (Acts 9:3ff.). Other times his approach is as gentle as a seed prying open its shell, grabbing the soil, and nudging toward the sunlight (Mark 4:3-20).

The varieties of our experience of Christ are evidence that a personality rather than a principle engages our attention. If a principle were making itself manifest in our lives, the pattern of experience would be more uniform. But Christ does not relate to all people the same way. Just as we open ourselves quickly to some individuals and slowly to others, so Christ varies how he discloses himself to us.

Although Christ's personality has priority over principle as the organizing force of reality, his personality does not exclude principle. The axiom by which Christ operates is that he is always seeking to save people.

Christ is the sculptor of salvation. He is the master of every medium: from the softwood of human relationships to the steel of political affairs. He is constantly carving, chiseling, melting, molding, hammering, shaping, and constructing new forms of healing and forgiveness. Sometimes Christ works in his home studio, the church. Other times he becomes a street artist and sets up shop wherever people work and play. Some of us feel more certain about Christ's art when it is practiced at his home studio rather than out in the world. In church we treasure the familiar tools of Christ's craft that are worn to the shape of his hands from so many years of use. When we hear the Scripture or sing a favorite hymn or respond to the sermon, we feel like Christ's own apprentice. His arm is about our shoulder, and with his own strength and skill he guides our uncertain efforts to remold our lives.

But sometimes Christ's work of salvation is not explicitly religious in context or content. We can pass by him at his workbench in the street and not even recognize that it is the same artisan plying his craft. Christ has deliberately laid aside his usual tools and smock in order to reach the public who will never enter his home studio. He is also there to help his apprentices who are supposed to be practicing in the world what he has taught them in his home. He comes dressed in a myriad of outfits: grandparents bearing smoked eel and Dutch almond cookies; a kind and generous aunt; a patient flute teacher. These are but one person's memories. If we examine our own experience closely, we discover that behind all our liberating and healing relationships works the master sculptor of salvation.

SALVATION THROUGH CHRIST'S POWER

Power can be brutal: one nation conquers another with its tanks and bombs. Power can be coercive: the government taxes its citizens. Power can be manipulative: one individual controls another. But power can also be a splendid, thrilling thing. There is the power of Beethoven's *Ninth Symphony* to send chills along our spine. The power of health returning to our bodies after a long illness. And above all, the power of loving individuals to make us into compassionate people.

Brutal, coercive, manipulative power holds the upper hand in human affairs. That at least is how things appear to the world. And unless they are religious Pollyannas, Christians also sometimes wonder if the world's dark view is not the truth. I most doubted Christ's power when I saw barbed wire and jagged glass along the top of a wall. A soldier with a semiautomatic rifle was at the gate. I walked into a barren little building and presented my passport to the guard who placed it, along with the money I was required to exchange, on a conveyor belt. He pushed a button, and the wafer-thin book and my West German marks were swallowed by some back room of officialdom. Two other tourists sat on steel chairs. No one spoke. It was not a place that prompted a person to say: *Guten Tag. Wie geht's?* Silence. Then the click of a switch and the hum of the conveyor belt bearing my passport and new money. The guard handed them to me, pointed to the door at the opposite end of the room from which I had entered, and I stepped outside into East Berlin.

I walked to Alexander Platz and had supper. The

power of Christ did not seem to be in the breaking
of bread that night. Then I caught a bus to spend
the evening with a young East Berlin pastor whose
parish was several miles from the wall.

Katherine opened the door almost instantly after
I knocked and welcomed me with her mellow blue
eyes and a smile. And that is how she responded all
evening to my questions: swinging open the door to
her life and ministry with spontaneous energy and
with the hospitality of a mind eager to share ideas
and experiences.

Sermons using marionettes and Biblical play-
scripts had attracted families to Katherine's
church. State officials, who were not happy at the
idea of making religion appealing, suggested that
she stick with tradition. For a while Katherine
dropped the puppets from the pulpit but later
resumed them. The next time she was cautioned
about her creative preaching, Katherine explained
that it had become a tradition in her church. Now
as I sat in her apartment she told me about a de-
lightful play-sermon on Jonah she was planning to
present.

Tennis fellowships had proved to be a way for
Katherine to establish a ministry with teen-agers.
Again she was questioned about how this related to
her traditional role as pastor. But using tact and
persistence, she made this too a "tradition" in her
church.

When a new high-rise apartment went up, Katherine started a house church there. She kept carving out a place for her ministry. She used every
resource she had—even the awkwardness which
people felt about her being a woman pastor. With
their typical German sensitivity to proper titles,
people were baffled when they could not refer to
their minister as *Herr* pastor. Katherine used their

inability to label her as a way to affirm her looser, creative style of ministry.

A political realist, Katherine had no illusion about the easy reunion of her separated homeland. But neither did she think of escaping to the West. She felt that Christ was giving her power to minister right where she was: four and a half kilometers from Alexander Platz in East Berlin.

It was eleven o'clock when I got up to leave. I remember looking at my watch because I was concerned that I would not make it back to West Berlin by midnight. Katherine assured me that if I stayed another half hour I could catch the last bus, which would drop me off near the gate with ten minutes to spare. I sat down. Katherine brought out cookies and tea, and fired off questions about the American political scene. The same mind that had talked about the power of Christ in her life and ministry now discussed the realities of the international power struggle. Katherine did not consider the two realms—Christ and the world—unrelated. It was Christ's power that sustained her hope despite the wall, despite the autocracy of the government, despite the conflict of the superpowers. There was about Katherine an interior confidence that reflected Paul's claim that "where the Spirit of the Lord is, there is freedom" (II Cor. 3:17).

Katherine and her ministry in the shadow of a wall are a sign of Christ's power in the world. Christ's power is the absolutely undemolishable hope that survives the most repressive measures. Christ's power is the creative imagination that presents the gospel in such refreshing ways that state authorities grow uneasy. Christ's power is the energy source that enables someone to minister to people under the most trying circumstances. Christ's power is the force that works through love

rather than through barbed wire and semiautomatic rifles. To the cynical world Christ's power
appears as the puny, foolish effort of a midget
against the giants of the earth. But to someone
whose heart is filled with that power, it is the ultimate force that shall tear down every wall and
shall endure forever after the last bullet is fired
and the last bomb dropped.

SALVATION THROUGH CHRIST'S PURPOSE

Everyone is a preacher, and every person's life is
a sermon to the world. Our pulpit is where we live
and work. Our congregation is made up of friends
and family, colleagues and strangers. Whatever
gospel we believe in we declare by our actions, our
words, our attitude. If it is the gospel of "me first
and all others second," the world will get the message. If it is the gospel of compassion and forgiveness, our congregation will feel the good news ra-
diating from us.

Many of us, however, are like the parson whose
sermon theme is vague and uncertain. The words
come tumbling out, but the thought is not sharp
and clear. We meander from point to point. For a
brief span the theme seems to be love, and our sermon shines into the hearts of our congregation. But
then we get sidetracked by doubt or bitterness, and
we seem to contradict what we said earlier. We as
well as our congregation become confused about
our purpose. And when at our life's end we step
down from the pulpit, we are disappointed in the
sermon we have preached. If only integrity, justice,
and truth could have sounded more consistently
and more clearly!

Jesus Christ *lived* the perfect sermon. Like the

best spoken sermons, Christ never let his life wander from its central focus: the Kingdom of God. Whether he was dealing with a sick person or someone needing forgiveness or a religious establishment tied up in its own laws or a petty governor worried about a riot, Jesus always kept his priorities straight. For him it was first things first. God's Kingdom: first. God's love: first. God's justice: first. God's truth: first. Everything else: second. Jesus had himself together because he organized his life around enduring truth.

Jesus was not content simply to proclaim love. He made his life one with his words. When a whore poured ointment on his feet, he loved her. When he saw a chiseling tax collector who ripped off his own people sitting in a sycamore tree, Jesus loved him. When he met his disciples on Easter after they had deserted him, he loved them. When he saw people so hungry that they could not make it home without fainting, he loved them. That constant, consistent love turned his life into a sermon of overwhelming power.

Jesus Christ is salvation because the purpose of his life can become the focus of our existence. By putting first things first, even as Christ did, our lives become coherent and meaningful. We no longer meander from love to doubt and bitterness. Our lives declare the same message as Christ: "Seek first [God's] kingdom and his righteousness, and all [other] things shall be yours as well" (Matt. 6:33).

SALVATION THROUGH CHRIST'S PRESENCE

Music, dance, and drama critics will sometimes say that a performer has "presence." By this term they mean something more than virtuosity or technique. They are describing the personal magnetism with which a performer draws the audience totally into what is happening on stage. There is no coughing or whispering in the auditorium because people are transformed by the creative action in which the artist immerses them. Presence is not taught in a conservatory. It is not printed on the page, nor is it applied in the dressing room. It is a quality of being that radiates from the artist and enraptures the audience.

The rhythm and the songfulness of the musician's performance become the pulse and the breath of the listeners. The dancer's buoyant, graceful motions make the soul to stand on tiptoe and pirouette. The actor's words invade the innermost sanctuary of the audience and reveal a truth that the listeners had hidden from everyone including themselves.

The experience of presence is salvation because it liberates the audience from the confines of its usual vision. The artist's presence brings into being a new creation, a new universe that includes elements of ecstasy and beauty that were previously missing from the listeners' lives.

Long after the finale, the artist's presence continues to be felt by the audience. The performance is remembered more as an event than as an entertainment. There is a sound that still echoes in the ear, a leap that still astounds the eye, a scene that still disturbs the psyche.

Jesus Christ is like that. He had presence with both enemies and admirers. When a mob was ready to throw him over a cliff, he walked right through the midst of them. When he spoke to crowds they were astounded by his authority. He mesmerized the common folk and intrigued the

sophisticated. To this very day his presence continues to haunt us. Like the Greeks who spoke to
Philip, "We wish to see Jesus" (John 12:21), we also
wish to penetrate to the mystery of his power, to the
secret of his grasp on the human imagination. Perhaps part of his presence was in his glance. The
Gospels often record how Jesus looked at people
with a special intensity (e.g., Mark 3:5, 34), but in
the last analysis, Christ's presence is a function of
something greater than any human characteristic.

Christ has presence because he is the most excit-
ing performer of God's music, the most graceful
dancer of heaven's ballet, the most impassioned
actor of the divine drama. The religious establishment of Christ's day knew every note in God's
score, but they sacrificed the soul of the music to a
literalistic interpretation. Theirs was not a performance that made people want to shout "Bravo,"
"Amen," or "Alleluia." But when Christ reached
out to people, they felt his presence. They sensed
that he was with them, beside them, and for them.
He was playing God's music so the rhythm was in
their feet and the melody was in their hearts.

Presence also has another, less dramatic meaning. It is the awareness that someone is concerned
about us even though that person is not with us. We
are married, and an old classmate cannot make the
wedding. We undergo surgery, and a dear friend
cannot be by our bedside. But we write afterward
to the person, "I felt your presence." The thought is
more than sentiment. It is our consciousness of love
that extends across time and space "like gold to
airy thinness beat" (John Donne). This is not the
stormy, virtuosic presence of the artist but the silent, steady caring of a friend.

Jesus Christ is salvation because he is the presence that both dazzles us with God's truth and stills

us with God's peace. The presence of Christ the
performer is revealed in the excitement of ideas. In
the creativity of artists. In the Gospel scenes between Jesus and the authorities. In the waves of joy
that break over us when we hear the "Hallelujah
Chorus." The presence of Christ our friend is
known in prayer. In silence. In meditation. In visits
and letters from people who care about us. In our
sense of well-being as we slip into a deep and soothing sleep. It is Christ's presence that makes us want
to cheer and clap our hands in a thunderous ova-
tion for the gift of life. It is also Christ's presence
that makes us as still as lovers who neither speak
nor touch because they are enjoying each other's
silent company.

FROM AWKWARDNESS TO AFFIRMATION

When we accept Jesus Christ as our Savior, the
greatest reality becomes the central truth of our
life. We feel ourselves connected to the essential
personal character of existence. We are energized
with power from the only undepletable source of
hope and love. Our life is filled with a clear and
compelling purpose. We sense the presence of one
who is always with us.

"Are you saved?" is no longer an awkward question. We now understand that it is not the mumbo
jumbo of an antiquated religious fraternity. It is a
question about the very nature of our life. It is a
way of asking: "Have you been liberated from what
holds you in bondage? Do you have a sense of security that can bear the earthquakes of war and tragedy? Have you ever felt the little world of yourself
rearranged by God's own hand into a new creation?
Have the dark ghosts that haunt the psyche been

driven from the closets of your soul? Have you ever
known the joy of being totally forgiven and accepted? Have you been healed? Have you felt the
strength of the resurrection in the face of death?
Have you framed your life with worship that
brings out the colors and shadings of daily existence?" These are the real-life issues that are
packed into the brief phrase "Are you saved?" To
read them all at once is overwhelming. We realize
that we shall never by ourselves be able to answer
Yes to the question of salvation. There is always
something about us that needs to be liberated or
healed or forgiven. If we are fiercely honest about
our own inadequacies, then our answer will be No.
No, we are not saved—at least not by ourselves.

But the answer to the nature of our existence
does not ultimately rest with ourselves. It lies in the
personality, the power, the purpose, the presence of
Jesus Christ. "He is the divine 'yes' " (II Cor. 1:19,
Phillips). While we can only say No, God in Jesus
Christ says Yes. Yes, we are liberated! Yes, we are
secure! Yes, we are created new! Yes, the demons
are gone! Yes, we are forgiven! Yes, we are healed!
Yes, the resurrection carries us through grief to
hope! Yes, worship frames our life!

Every single Yes is unconditional. It will never
be turned into a No or modified into Maybe. Every
Yes is guaranteed not by our own word but by God's
word: Jesus Christ. He is the divine "Yes." He is the
answer to the question of salvation. By the power of
his being, yes, we are saved. Yes, today. Yes, tomorrow. Yes, forever and ever. For "every promise of
God finds its affirmative in him, and through him
can be said the final Amen, to the glory of God" (II
Cor. 1:20, Phillips).